YEARS
ON THE
PATH

YEARS

ON THE

PATH

ESSAYS BY

JEANETTE STOKES

FORWARD BY RACHAEL WOOTEN

The Resource Center for Women
& Ministry in the South, Inc.

Durham, North Carolina

Copies of this book may be ordered from:
The Resource Center for Women and Ministry in the South, Inc.
1202 Watts Street
Durham, North Carolina 27701
919-683-1236
rcwmsnc@aol.com
www.rcwms.org

CONTENTS

For the young women:
Jenny, Meghan, Candice, Sarah, Candace, and Erin.

You are the ones who will carry on the work
in feminism and religion in the future.

Here's to the next 35 years!

FOREWORD

By all rights, Jeanette Stokes and I should have met in 1977 when
we were both completely taken up with creating nonprofits to serve
women's critical needs. As a freshly-minted seminary graduate, Jeanette
was in Durham, North Carolina, laying the groundwork for the
Resource Center for Women and Ministry in the South (RCWMS).
As a freshly-minted PhD in psychology, I had signed on to become a
founding mother of the Women's Center in Raleigh, North Carolina,
the brainchild of Sister Evelyn Mattern.

During the 1980s, working with women in my psychotherapy practice,
I realized that women's spiritual development played a central role in
their healing process. I overheard friends at Pullen Memorial Baptist
Church discussing conferences organized by someone named Jeanette
Stokes and RCWMS. I wondered, who was she, and who were these
women in ministry? In the early 1990s, visiting friends in Black
Mountain, North Carolina, I noticed an edition of *South of the Garden*,
the RCWMS newsletter, in their magazine rack. "Maybe I should
subscribe," I thought at the time. But the thought passed until 1997,
when I returned to Raleigh after completing three years of studies at the
Jung Institute in Zurich, Switzerland.

Ultimately, it was Sr. Evelyn who brought us together. Shortly after I
returned from Zurich I reconnected with Evelyn. She invited me to a
meeting of her Durham colleagues who gathered regularly to meditate
and explore the possibility of creating an interfaith monastery. Having
devoted as much time to the study and practice of Tibetan Buddhism as
to my Jungian studies, my heart lit up.

I met Jeanette at this interfaith gathering and immediately wanted
to spend more time with her and learn about the Resource Center.
She explained that RCWMS was moving away from sponsoring large
conferences featuring nationally recognized feminist theologians. Small
workshops and retreats with local talent as leaders were taking center
stage. At the same time, Jeanette's spiritual interests were widening. "I

take support from people in other denominations, other faiths, other traditions. I like interfaith settings these days," she wrote in a 2000 essay, which was included in *25 Years in the Garden*.

Jeanette writes unequivocally about this development in the current volume, in her 2010 essay, "Where am I Now?" She explains, "Although feminist Christianity is my spiritual home, my life and work have carried me beyond, outside, and around the corner from exclusive Christianity.... I do not need or want to be with people of faith who are only like me."

During this same period, writing became a central focus of the creative mission of the organization. In 2002, Nancy Peeler Keppel and her family foundation began a series of gifts to RCWMS to fund a writing program, which grew to include week-long women's writing retreats, weekend writing workshops, and a yearly essay contest. The winning essays were published alongside Jeanette's well-loved work in *South of the Garden*.

Jeanette's commentaries stimulate our thinking. In the forward to the first collection of her essays Mary Hunt declares, "Jeanette Stokes has created the genre of feminist inspirational writing."

Jeanette's writing also reminds me of feminist literary criticism in which the critic writes about her life alongside her assessment of the literature she reviews. The writer introduces herself to the reader, acknowledging that who she is necessarily influences her opinion. She refuses to claim intellectual objectivity or superiority. The feminist offers her critique in a related way to the reader.

Jeanette does this in every essay. She often writes as a critic—of the institutional church, of political institutions, of racial and gender biases, among other things. But first she places herself squarely in the material. This is who I am; this is why I'm writing this today; this is how I feel. Like other feminist critics, Jeanette explains her connection to the topic, building intimacy with her reader by revealing both her thoughts and feelings. She shows up on the page as she does in life—exuberant, curious, and confident.

Contemplating the interrelatedness of all things in the universe lies at the core of Buddhist practice. In Tibetan practices, images are used as objects of meditation and as teaching devices. The images actually contain the teachings. Tara, the beloved female buddha of Tibet, appears as the first image of feminism in the tradition. She embodies the teachings on the relationship between Buddhist wisdom and compassion, including compassionate action. In particular, she is the first figure in the tradition who speaks up for the spiritual needs of women.

RCWMS has sponsored many workshops and events related to Tara, allowing me to share her story and her wisdom in a relaxed interfaith setting. I love recounting the ancient story of Tara's origins in this context. Tara's wit, courage, and motivation closely resemble Jeanette's approach when she founded the Resource Center.

In a much earlier lifetime (when she was known as the young woman, Yeshe Dawa, or Wisdom Moon), Tara was advised by a group of monks to pray to be reborn as a man. She was so advanced in her practice, they urged, that she would instantly become enlightened. The only thing she lacked was a male body. Tara reminded them that enlightened consciousness was not limited by their cultural concepts of gender. Ultimate reality contains all things, male and female alike, and cannot be understood as one or the other. As human beings are manifestations of this consciousness, gender limitations could not possibly be relevant in the quest for awakening.

In the next moment, Tara vowed that she would only become enlightened in a woman's body, and that she would work in her female form throughout time to free all beings from suffering. She was well aware of the obstacles that women faced in receiving spiritual education and proper ordination, tremendous obstacles that still exist today.

Jeanette's motivations for starting the Resource Center remind me of Tara's vow. In the months after graduating from Duke Divinity School, Jeanette was fully cognizant of the obstacles that women in ministry faced in obtaining jobs or attaining voice and standing in their communities. She knew that women were having a rough time, and she set out to alleviate the suffering she knew would be part of their path.

Courageous women like Jeanette have a way of creating joy in their wake as they go about creating opportunities for women and men by virtue of their thoughtful actions, whether these actions occur in the pulpit, in the larger world, or through the written word.

The words that fill the essays in this volume, replete with insight, humor, wisdom, and compassion, awaken us to the possibilities inherent in each moment. Jeanette teaches us the glory of slowing down and paying attention to the beautiful details of the world around us and the worlds within us. When we look deeply, as she does, into the moments of our lives, which contain the intricate gestures of giving and receiving with all the beings we encounter, insight arises.

Through our looking and seeing, understanding and writing, we hold these moments and relationships delicately. We make them sacred.

In these essays, Jeanette calls forth a sense of the sacred and offers that to us. She inspires us to follow in her footsteps. To look, to see, to share, to write, to treasure our lives. By doing so, we return to her Garden and to the Garden of the Divine Feminine, again and again.

Rachael Wooten
Raleigh, North Carolina
Summer 2012

PREFACE

It is hard to believe that ten years have gone by since the publication of *25 Years in the Garden*, the first collection of my essays from *South of the Garden*, the newsletter of the Resource Center for Women and Ministry in the South.

In these pages, you will find comments about my relationship to writing. Producing essays for *South of the Garden* actually helped me to think of myself as a writer. I have even arranged my schedule to allow time to write, and some days I actually do it.

Writing the text of a book is only the beginning of making a book. In my case, it took a village to actually produce the volume you are holding in your hands.

I designed and laid out the pages of *25 Years in the Garden* with lots of help from friends who are professionals in the business. I found it both rewarding and exhausting, so I did several things to ease the production of *35 Years on the Path*. I began collecting my essays from *South of the Garden* in a file by themselves about five or six years ago. Then two or three years ago I started laying them out so they looked like a book. When the time came to produce the book, part of the work was already done.

Jeanne Taylor and her wonderful staff at Designing Solutions in Durham, North Carolina, did a great job coming up with a cover that would be compatible with the earlier book but that has its own personality. The title and the labyrinth image on the cover suggest that the work of RCWMS—and life itself—are long and winding paths. One thing I love about the labyrinth is that it has a destination, which the walker will reach if she stays on the path. In life, I believe that walking one's own path is the destination, in and of itself.

If there are any errors in this volume, it's not for lack of amazingly talented people who tried to spot my mistakes and correct them. Since

I was the last one to have my hand on the files before printing, there is simply no telling what creative mistakes I may have added.

I am deeply grateful to all the people who helped to edit these essays, especially Mary Coffman, Andrea Davis, Meghan Florian, Pat Green, Wakoh Shannon Hickey, Amy Kellum, Michael Kellum, Marcy Litle, Kaudie McLean, Ron Moss, Lori Pistor, Mary Russell Roberson, Nancy Rosebaugh, Sarah Walls, my wonderful RCWMS colleague Jennifer McGovern, and countless others who accidentally came by our office or sent me an email when I was in an editing panic.

I also want to thank the people I turn to when I have a knotty grammar or punctuation problem. I wonder whether there will be any humans in the future who understand the ins and outs of English grammar. Emily Seelbinder and Carolyn Park Currie have been kind enough to help me out when I have found myself in a tangle. I have no idea how these wizards keep all the rules in their heads. Though they may occasionally consult the *Chicago Manual of Style*, they are sharp enough to know when they need to.

People who are good proofreaders must have a special gene. My mother has it, but she didn't pass it on to me. One of my problems is that I'm not a great speller, so you can slip any number of errors by me and I'll just imagine them as words that fit. Not so with a crack proofreader. Special thanks go to Margie Hattori and Liz Dowling-Sendor for being the final readers of these pages. Thank you for sharing your sharp eyes with me.

It is my hope that these kind friends and I have created a book that will be a good companion to you. My only request is that after you read it, please give a copy to a young adult woman so that she might carry on the work of weaving feminism and spirituality into a vision of a justice for the world.

Jeanette Stokes
Durham, North Carolina
Summer 2012

ICE

We had an amazing ice storm here in central North Carolina in early December. Tree limbs down everywhere, streets blocked, more than a million people without power. Some spent a day in the dark and cold, some a whole week. For my neighborhood it was three days.

I was at the office working on a fundraising letter when the snow started Wednesday afternoon. When I called the local copy shop to see about making some prints, they said they were closing, "Right now!" In the late afternoon, I drove the six blocks to my house. The snow had turned to freezing rain. Glazed trees and power lines had begun to sparkle like glass figurines.

The coating of ice thickened through the evening and the lights went out about 10:30 p.m. The sound of crashing tree limbs woke me off and on all night. Flashes of red and blue light filled the sky as transformers blew out. Block by block, Raleigh, Durham, and Chapel Hill went dark.

My house had no heat, lights, phone, or hot water. I did have a fireplace and gas burners on my stove, battery power in my computer, and one small radio. The really lucky thing was that I had stocked up on wood about ten days before the storm. Some people had fireplaces but no wood.

Thursday night was so dark without the glow of streetlights and the constant flashing of the caution light at the end of my block. I could see the stars in the sky over the city as never before. It was hard to read after dark, even with lots of candles burning. That must be why evening reading was not a favorite pastime before electricity. To keep warm, I doubled up the quilts on the bed and ate a lot of soup. I got tired of cheese sandwiches, but that was about my only complaint.

The ice storm made everything stop. Since I had had a particularly busy fall, it was a real gift to have my whole world come to a screeching halt.

I rather enjoyed sitting by the fire, being more or less stuck at home, and not having the phone ring very much until the power came back on.

GROCERIES

My neighborhood grocery store was without power for several days. The frozen and refrigerated sections were moved to a storage unit with a generator, for safekeeping. The lights and cash registers were, obviously, not working. On the second or third day of the power outage, store managers pushed open their electric sliding doors to customers with cash.

I arrived with a friend who, God bless him, had $40 in his pocket. (I never carry cash. Don't believe in the stuff.) We waited outside for our turn.

An employee escorted each customer through the store. Our escort, a patient man named Neal, wrote down each item and its price on a piece of paper.

When there is no electricity, and no telling how long that will be the case, everything in a grocery store is a temptation. Chocolate! We restrained ourselves, buying sensible items—milk, eggs, cheese, soup, and fruit.

When we had gathered our items in a basket, Neal escorted us to the front of the store where another employee was operating a hand-held calculator. Slowly the cashier totaled our bill. We paid in cash.

As I left the store, I felt like kissing the manager's feet.

WEDDING

Len and Charles had been planning their early December wedding for months. Both in their fifties, they had created an event to please themselves and their community. A week before the wedding, I got an e-mail from Len with complicated directions for driving to the downtown church where the happy event was to take place. The city was planning an outdoor celebration for the same day, same time, in the same part of town. "Light Up Durham" was going to be in the way. "Having dealt with this snafu, I'm sure the wedding will come off without a hitch," Len said at the end of her note.

Enter the ice storm, three days before the wedding. Power went out at the church. Power went out at the reception site. On the day of the wedding, the wedding and the reception were moved to a downtown hotel that had a generator.

Friends called wedding guests to announce the change. Others pitched in to decorate a ballroom in the hotel. Flowers from a fancy dinner at the hotel the night before were donated for the tables. The power outage meant "Light Up Durham" was cancelled, so no alternate routes were needed for driving downtown.

The wedding was lovely and full of warmth. The bride wore red satin and wedding guests in turn shared what they had learned about love.

When the power was finally restored, I straightened up my house. As I moved books, blankets, coats, newspapers, and teacups from the hearth, I felt a little sadness. I was going to miss the warm nest I had built within the fire's warmth.

I was glad for the experience and had a new appreciation for things I take for granted most days. The little things. I flip a switch at night and light comes on bright enough for these aging eyes to read a book. I turn the tap and in a matter of moments warm water soothes cold hands. I rise on a bright twenty-degree day and my house is as warm as I like. I enjoy these gifts of the modern world. If we can restore these simple pleasures to millions of people in a week, you would think we could figure out how to deliver some modicum of justice and peace.

Some people complained about the inconvenience of the storm and others really did suffer from the cold. I tried to enjoy it. Life became very simple—keep the fire going, boil water, heat soup, and try to keep warm. I loved sitting by the fire, staring into the flames. I wonder why it so hard to sit there when the power is on.

Volume 24, Number 1, January 2003

SEEDS

I almost always rush to my 5:30 yoga class on Wednesday afternoons. I mean to leave my office at 5:00, drive the short mile to Yoga Spot, and have plenty of time to roll out my mat, stretch, and calm myself before Claudia instructs me in becoming a human pretzel.

I left my office at 4:00 on a Wednesday afternoon in September to stop at Not Just Paper, the local paper outlet. I've learned to allow extra time there in case I get lost in the shelves of beautiful recycled paper, jars of colored pens, or stacks of paper plates. This time it was the wrapping paper that got me, rolls and rolls for only a dollar each. I meditated on whether to buy four or forty? How long can a person look at rolls of wrapping paper before she figures out there are only six different designs? How many rolls is it necessary to examine after that? You either get all six or multiples of the ones you like. It's not like solving a differential equation. You shouldn't have to stare at it for hours before a pattern emerges.

But there I was. I even went in the back and asked if there was more wrapping paper. "Oh, yes, lots more," the woman said enthusiastically as she showed me to the area of the warehouse where it was stored. "Why is it so cheap?" I asked. "Because we have so much of it." I took Economics in college. I know the theory of supply and demand, but I didn't think anyone followed it any more. (Do you know that some research outfit actually tried to find a pattern in the prices for airline tickets and they could not find one! Random. The prices were totally random.)

"Do you have any Christmas paper?" I asked as the clerk added up my five rolls. Two of the big white daisies on blue background, two of the metallic butterflies (Jewel will like that one on her fiftieth birthday present this week), and one of the subdued beige with flowers in case I was invited to what, a sad baby shower? "We have it on order," said the enthusiastic woman helping me.

By then it was 4:50 p.m. I had to make a choice. I could either rush back to my office to close it up and get my briefcase or I could go to yoga in a leisurely fashion as I always intend to.

That particularly Wednesday I had promised myself that I would move slowly all day. I had, in fact, spent ten minutes on the sofa after lunch. So, I proudly made the decision not to go by my office but to go straight to yoga. The seed store, Stone Bros. & Byrd, is right across the street from Yoga Spot. I made a little detour to buy grass seed. So much for getting to yoga early.

Stone Bros. is a business establishment that ought to be protected by the endangered species act. It still has people who can answer your questions and a cash register with a bell. "What are you recommending about planting grass seed in this drought?" I asked the man who, in my mind, owns the place. "Here's what I'm telling people...." Oh, right, other people have noticed the drought. I listen politely to his good advice about punching deep holes in the yard, something I never intend to do. I pay a teenager to mow and can't in my wildest dreams imagine being able to talk him into "aerating." My yard will have to survive without holes. I don't even care if the birds eat all the grass seed. I just plant it once a year.

"How big is the yard? Is it as big as this room?" asks the owner. "Are you kidding? I live over in Trinity Park. My lot is 50 x 150 feet, and it has a house, a garage, a garden, and sidewalks on it." "Three pounds should do it," he says as he shows me the five-pound bag we both agree is too much.

Now the question is which kind of seed? Shade? Sun? "Mixed," I say. "Plush something," says he. It is only fifty cents more than the other one that I don't know anything about. I begin to wonder if like Alice I will ever emerge from Wonderland. Three something, he writes on a long thin sheet of paper. I'm not going to get grass seed after all. I'm going to get blotter seed. What am I supposed to do? Go home, chew up the paper, and spit it out on the yard? "Lime?" he asks. "Oh, yeah," I say. I'm supposed to spread that around every year and I think it has been five. "Yes, pellet lime." I hate the powdered stuff, when you try to spread it around it goes everywhere, like powdered sugar. "I can spread it with my spreader, right?" I ask. (Well, it's not exactly my spreader, even though it lives in my shed. It belongs to Mr. Wheless next door, but he is eighty-five and he hasn't asked about it in years. I don't bother to explain this part.)

Lime, he writes on the same piece of paper. I'm catching onto the system. I pay for the seed and lime and am sent to the "back" to see Amos, to whom I present my long thin piece of paper. "Grass seed," he says. I wait for the weighing to begin. Amos approaches a scale that seems older than either of us. He removes the weight on the left side of the scale and replaces it with the three-pound weight. On the right side of the scale he places a small brown paper bag, open at the top. He scoops seed from an open bin and pours it slowly into the bag until the scale balances. He folds the top of the bag over twice, pulls a piece of twine off a spool, makes a double loop around the bag, ties a knot, breaks the line with his hand, and presents the bag to me.

Something deep inside of me let out a great sigh. I was as delighted as the child 100 years ago who was allowed to select the calico sack of flour her family would take home, or the tiny boy who was entrusted with a precious bag of sugar. What a blessing it was, that simple ritual, performed at an old table, in the back of a seed store, in an extra moment of time.

Volume 24, Number 1, January 2003

TREE

I dread taking down the Christmas tree. It's a lot of trouble and it makes me sad. I always love my Christmas tree. I've put up a tree of my own each year since I moved into my first apartment after graduate school. The first one was a fluffy pine, decorated with homemade gingham and calico ornaments and fabric bows. Eventually, I switched to Fraser firs because they have more space between the branches for the ever-growing collection of ornaments.

This year I marched out Thanksgiving weekend and selected a tree. It usually takes three or four trips to the Christmas tree lot to get a tree. The first trip is on foot, a side-trip from my daily walk around Duke's East Campus. I go back in my car to pay for the tree. It usually takes two trips with a friend in a truck to get the tree. The first time the lot is invariably closed. This year I accomplished all this just before the ice storm, so the tree spent several happy days in my cold house soaking up the water in its stand.

The tree stood there naked for two full weeks before an anticipated gathering at my house prompted me to put lights and ornaments on it. I was so discombobulated by the ice storm that I don't know when I would have gotten the tree if I had not done it so early this year.

I enjoyed the tree all through Christmas and New Year's. I photographed it, as I do every year. I was sure that it was the most beautiful tree I had ever had. Such a pleasing shape. I can't imagine why the pictures of my trees all look alike.

I left the tree up through Epiphany (January 6) and on January 7 the narcissus Mary Margaret had given me flung themselves out of their red glass bowl and crashed to the ground, announcing it was time to start putting away Christmas decorations. It was time to start letting go of the tree.

Some years I cry. This year on January 9, in anticipation of another gathering at my house, I steeled myself to take down the tree. I went slowly and with great care. I put Krishna Das (Hindu chants) on the CD player (let's get another religion going here and get off Christmas). I told each ornament how much I loved it and recalled its history.

My favorite ornaments are fabric-covered Styrofoam balls that I decorated Thanksgiving weekend 1964. I was thirteen. My father had left my mother (and me) that year. Sally Patton's family invited Mother and me to go to Arkansas for Thanksgiving. (Sally has been my best friend since I was three years old.) The Pattons had a ranch, a place on the White River in Arkansas. Mrs. Patton took along a box of fabric, rickrack, and sequins for making ornaments. Every year when I remove these balls from the tree, I remember how good it felt to be gathered up by the Pattons. Decades later I understand how vulnerable I was at that moment and how much the kindness of friends meant to me. My attachment to these particular ornaments is proof enough.

This year when I finished removing the lights and ornaments and tipped the tree over to drag it out of the house, it occurred to me that this could be a new holiday, "The Dragging of the Tree." It could at least be part of a carol along with, "The rising of the sun, and the running of the deer."

Given enough time and attention, the dragging of the tree does not have to be so painful. Change is hard, transitions stressful. I resist the falling of autumn leaves as much as clearing out the Christmas tree. But just as the falling leaves yield a more open sky, taking down the tree lets more light and space into my house. The New Year's impulse to clear out can take hold. The dragging of the tree marks yet another point on the ever-turning wheel of the year.

As I contemplated this year's tree in the last days before taking it down, I recognized it to be a big warm benevolent presence, a Great Mother. Welcoming, delicious smelling, full of kindness, it's like a big mama.

Christmas trees are descended from the circles of trees that formed the groves of the goddess. I came to think of the tree as a winter solstice goddess tree. No wonder I was reluctant to take it out of my house. No wonder dismantling the tree went better with the extra care and attention any sacred object deserves.

Volume 24, Number 1, January 2003

BUNNY

I love Easter. I am crazy about the Easter Bunny, and I love brightly colored eggs so much that most of the year I have a big blue bowl of aging Easter eggs on my dining room table. Did you know that if you let boiled eggs sit around long enough the innards dry up? If you shake one of these old eggs, it sounds like a small rubber ball is rattling around inside.

My friend Allan is the Easter Bunny, or E. Bunny as he signs his cards. Each year, he dyes eggs and delivers them to his friends. Another friend, Jewel, is one of the people who helps the bunny dye eggs. I always thought we were talking about a couple dozen eggs and that the bunny needed help because the dyeing process was complicated. Wrong. When I saw Jewel at a lecture on the night before Easter, she said the list of recipients has grown to 110 people. At five eggs per person, that's over 500 eggs!

I left a snack out for the bunny this year. It takes him hours and hours in the middle of the night to make his rounds. Jewel said he gets overwhelmed with all the candy people leave for him, so I made a cheese sandwich, sliced an apple, and left them in a bag by the front door. I went to bed that night in great anticipation of the dawn and a gift of new eggs.

When I got up Sunday morning and opened the front door, there were no eggs. The cheese sandwich was untouched. "Maybe the bunny ran out of gas, broke down, or ran out of eggs," I thought and worried that the bunny had taken on too much. That will teach me to count my eggs before the bunny brings them.

Disappointment is not an attractive feeling. "Don't be so selfish," I told myself. "I'm sure a lot of wonderful people got eggs. What do you need with more eggs? You already have a whole beautiful bowl full of eggs." But disappointed I was all the same. Not angry, not hurt, just disappointed.

I checked the front door every twenty minutes, just in case the bunny was running late. Each time I opened the door I expected eggs. No eggs appeared but other things did. A gorgeous potted lavender plant arrived that I suspected was from my sweetie. Lovely, but where in the world was that bunny?

Another time when I opened the door I found a small purple sack with two eggs I recognized from previous Easters. Perhaps the bunny ran out of eggs and I got recycled ones, I thought. Stiff upper lip, recycled eggs are better than no eggs at all. A neighbor called about that time to say that she had left these two, but not to eat them because they were old. Okay, those were a bonus, what happened to the real deal? I put the bunny's cheese sandwich back in the refrigerator and went off to church.

Church was full of the usual delights—children, friends, music, flowers—and since it was an extra-long service, I managed to forget nearly everything about everything. That afternoon I went to my studio and made art. Soft spring air drifted in through the screen door as I happily glued paper onto book board to make covers for blank books. When I finally went home in the late afternoon I was actually surprised to find at my door a basket filled with real grass, red clover blossoms, and five beautiful eggs. They were deep jewel colors—red, orange, yellow, green, and blue. My little heart went flip-flop. "The bunny didn't forget me, he didn't forget me!" Along with the basket there was a jar of pansies and a note of apology.

When I put the whole collection on my table, it was so gorgeous that I took pictures. It looked like a party—a pot of lavender, a big bowl of eggs, a purple sack, a jar of pansies, and a basket with the five most beautiful eggs in the world.

Sometimes I'm not sure how I feel about the crucifixion and resurrection, but I am sure about the Easter Bunny. One man loves his friends so much that he dyes 500 eggs, drives around all night to deliver them, and makes an extra effort for the one he forgot.

Volume 24, Number 2, May 2003

HOME

Anita McLeod led a wonderful workshop on wisdom and menopause for RCWMS in January. In talking about what women need, she mentioned how important it is for a woman to have a room of her own. I noticed that even though I live in a house by myself, I don't have a room of my own. What's the matter with this picture?

I have a room that was always supposed to be my room. It's a small upstairs study with big windows overlooking a park. In it there was a loveseat, desk, filing cabinet, bookcase, and two extra chairs. I had often imagined a comfortable reading chair and footstool where the loveseat sat. I even kept a tattered old footstool in the garage in service of this vision, but never did anything to change the room.

After the menopause workshop, I remembered I had received not one, but two e-mails from Katie, the new associate at the church I attend, begging for a sofa or loveseat for her office. I'd had a feeling the e-mails (sent to the whole church) were somehow meant for me. Now I was convinced, so I wrote her and asked if she was still in need. She was and agreed to line up a truck and a helper and move the loveseat out. I decided I could bring my favorite chair home from my office, recover the footstool, and create a room of my own.

And that's what happened. Katie moved the loveseat. I took the footstool to a friendly upholsterer and selected a nice medium blue from his stock of leftover fabric. I shoved my blue-checked chair in the trunk of my car and hauled it to my house. I added one small bookcase, removed the extra chairs and voilà, a room of my own. The room contains just the essential elements, a good reading chair and the writing desk I bought a decade ago with money I made from selling an old piano. I don't make music. I do write. It was a good trade.

I can sit at the desk and write in my journal or sit in the chair and gaze out the windows. One night in April I turned the lights off in the house, sat in the blue-checked chair, put my feet up on the footstool, and gazed out at the soft night. It was what I had wanted. It was a view on the world, as Christopher Alexander would say. Humans like to have a view on the world. Christopher Alexander's *A Pattern Language* is full of little tidbits about what makes humans feel comfortable in buildings.

I had wanted to get rid of the loveseat for years. It is perfectly gorgeous, but neither serviceable nor comfortable. It was too big for the tiny room. It wound up holding piles of paper and Christmas presents that I couldn't figure out where to put.

My former husband helped pick out the loveseat and made sure it matched the art and the rug. It looked perfect. Making the house look perfect was one of his favorite projects, and I was often what got in the way. I was accustomed to this, though, because my mother had always made everything look just right. To this day her house looks like someone from *House & Garden* is about to arrive to photograph it. My mother had a messy child: me. It does not matter that I'm not all that messy, I'm just messier than she is.

I've been living in my house by myself for over five years, and I've been pretty slow about making changes. I think I was afraid I'd mess it up. I can't ever make things look as perfect as my mother or my former husband. But they don't live here. I do. My job is to make changes that please me.

A recent change was the mattress on my bed. It wore out. When I got out of bed in the morning, there was a big dip where I had been. So, in December, I bought a new one, and I love it. It's very thick. Soft on the top and firm inside. That was pretty easy. The mattress situation had become rather desperate.

In January I refinanced my house in order to take advantage of the falling interest rates. I now own a mortgage by myself for the first time in my life. It occurs to me that what has been happening this year is that I've been taking possession of my own house. I've lived in the house for nearly a dozen years. I don't know who I thought it belonged to.

It's like that with life sometimes. Living in one's own life is not as easy as it sounds. I once heard someone say that the task of aging is taking possession of one's own soul. I'm taking up residence in my house and in my life. If moving furniture helps with this process, then so be it.

Life is a journey and I'm on my way home.

Volume 24, Number 2, May 2003

LIGHT

It is early September and my body remembers the light.

I was twenty-one the summer Mr. Bainbridge pointed out to me the special quality of the light in September. We were standing in his front yard in Chatham, Massachusetts, in the early evening just after Labor Day. "I love the light this time of year," he said.

I don't think I had paid much attention to the way the light changed over the seasons except to notice that I did not like that it got dark so early in the winter in Massachusetts. I'd leave an afternoon lab at my college at 5:00 p.m, and find the world pitch dark outside.

I paused that evening thirty years ago to try to see what Mr. Bainbridge saw—the quality, the angle of the light. I remember him almost every year when the light changes. This year it was on the second day of September. After a hot hazy week and a rainy Labor Day weekend, the air cleared. I was driving through a neighborhood in Raleigh, North Carolina, about 6:00 in the evening when I noticed the light.

The world looked washed and fresh, not steamed and limp like it had in mid-summer. The warm light made the trees bright against a clear blue sky. Houses looked cheerful and skyscrapers sparkled like shiny toys in the distance.

Things look hopeful in this light. The liriope boasts hundreds of proud purple wands. The school year starts. Meetings and work projects crank up again. Full of hope, I picked the first of September as my wedding day some years ago.

Summer's close is bittersweet. I savor the last of the local corn, peaches, and blueberries. Cool temperatures and gentle light bring renewed life to the garden. The zinnias bloom frantically. Grapes ripen on the vine. One last cluster of blossoms opens on my favorite rosebush. Fall and loss are in the air.

Dappled light falls across my journal pages in the morning just like it did in September 1997 as I recorded with shock the breakup of my marriage. A prism in the east window splashes rainbow fragments across the wall in front of me just as it did on that unthinkable morning of September 11, 2001.

The late summer song of the cicadas suggests the gentle snoring of a giant or the rise and fall of an ocean of dry leaves. The purple coneflowers stand dying in the garden, feeding their seeds to the goldfinches, as they must have in those other Septembers.

Abundant summer rains have left the grass quite green, but it won't be for long. My sidewalk is already strewn with fallen leaves.

My body remembers the light of other years with sadness or relief. The angle of the light reminds me that life is a never-ending spiral of endings and beginnings.

Volume 24, Number 3, September 2003

PATH

I thought falling in love would save me. It didn't. I fell in love with my husband and he with me, with Kate Wolfe's "Give Yourself to Love" playing in the background, but it didn't save us from heartbreak or from breaking up.

Falling in love isn't the answer to anything. Don't get me wrong, falling in love is a lovely experience, but in some ways it is like eating chocolate cake. Once the cake is eaten, you have to go back to your regular life, your regular self, and all the ways you may be unhappy about any of that.

In September 1997 I found myself at a crossroads. My marriage was falling apart, I was making a canvas labyrinth, and I was about to resume my work at the Resource Center for Women and Ministry in the South after a two-and-a-half-year break. I've often wondered about the coincidence of these events. At one point I fussed at God, saying that it was not an even trade—my marriage for a labyrinth and a job.

It wasn't a trade, of course. It was an intersection, a place where my inner and outer journeys met. Let me explain.

I had been unhappy for some time. At first I thought it was my work, so I quit my job as Executive Director of RCWMS in April 1995. The work had come to feel boring and demanding, the way pushing a pea across the floor with my nose might be. I was pretty good at pushing the pea, but I was really tired of it. Directing a small, perpetually under-funded nonprofit organization can be wearing. Ask any of the droves of good people in this country who do it. I was not unusual. I was just tired, as anyone would have been. And I was surprised.

I had always thought that by inventing my own work I could insure that I'd love it forever. I thought creating an organization I adored would save me from burnout. I was wrong. After almost eighteen years at RCWMS, I could no longer muster any enthusiasm. The spark had gone out.

Once I left the Resource Center, I rested for several months, trying to do only those things I really wanted to do and sitting still when I didn't know what I wanted. After this period, which I refer to as my sabbatical, I rented an office, made a lot of art, and began working again.

It wasn't long before I realized I was recreating the work I had done for RCWMS, only without the organization. I was writing, teaching, and planning workshops. It seems to be the work I do. In 1997 when the Board suggested my returning to my old job, it made sense.

When I returned to RCWMS in September 1997, I hoped for a slightly different focus. I was tired of planning large conferences with well-known outside speakers. I was hungry for something a little more intimate. I wanted to offer to others some of what I was learning about taking care of my own spirit. Now our workshops are smaller and more often focus on spirituality. We have developed a program on writing and offer the labyrinth as a form of walking meditation.

I fell in love with the labyrinth at Grace Cathedral on a trip to San Francisco in 1996. That labyrinth is a replica of a twelfth century stone one laid into the floor of Chartres Cathedral in France. The first time I walked the labyrinth, I knew I wanted to share it with others. Since portable canvas labyrinths cost about $3,500, I decided to make one. How hard could it be to stitch up at forty-by-forty-foot canvas floor cloth and paint a winding purple path on it? Hard but fun. One hundred eighty hours of stitching, drawing, and painting later, voilà, a gorgeous canvas replica I could take almost anywhere.

My friend Brian asked me recently what I learned by working with the labyrinth. Without thinking, I said that the labyrinth was a path that had taken me where I needed to go. Where was that? It took me to France, to the cathedral at Chartres, to a medieval understanding of God as the center of everything. It taught me about a time in Europe before the Reformation and the Enlightenment when the cycles of life and the seasons of the year were central metaphors.

European cathedrals, though huge in area, can be intimate spaces filled with a rich mixture of intoxicating sights, sounds, and smells. Small chapels, tapestries, paintings, incense, candles, bells, and a healthy dose of the unknown suggest the presence of the holy. These often dark, sometimes damp, somewhat mysterious places provide a culture in which even a modern imagination and sense of wonder can grow.

An altar in a European cathedral is often laden with flowers and candles. A statue of Mary might be brightly painted or lovingly dressed in rich fabrics of silk or velvet. For all the ways she may have been used and abused, Mary is still a feminine presence in Catholicism. She lives in the hearts of people all over the world. The liturgy calls her the Mother of God. Though popes and priests would deny it, she is the Great Mother of ancient religions. She is all but missing from Protestantism today.

The Protestant Reformation threw out most of the appealing sensory elements of worship. In an attempt to replace devotion to images with devotion to the word, the Reformers threw the baby out with the bath water, or to be more exact, they threw the mother out with the bath water.

It was the labyrinth that helped me notice that the feminine divine was missing from American Protestant churches. The labyrinth took me to European cathedrals as well as a number of large American churches. I noticed the absence of the feminine even in an ornate gothic-style church like Duke University Chapel where I take the labyrinth at least once a year.

The labyrinth's softly curving path leads only to its own center, to a simple rose shape, a medieval icon for Mary. Walking the labyrinth caused me to remember Mary and to long for the feminine divine. It offered me an experience of intimacy with God that reminds me of the gentle connection between a mother and child.

The labyrinth is an amazing container. Walking the labyrinth provides a way to hold and to feel whatever is going on. If walking the labyrinth feels hard, it's usually because life feels hard. If it feels light and playful, it's because I feel playful. If it is sad, it is because I feel sad. Walking the labyrinth is an opportunity to experience God walking with us. The theological term for that is immanence. In quietly walking the labyrinth, we can open to the possibility of experiencing the presence of God.

By the time my marriage fell apart in 1997, I had almost lost track of myself. Perhaps it was from trying, somewhat unsuccessfully, to please my mate. Perhaps it was the normal wear and tear of living with another human being. I had come to think of myself as a small brown bird. I had lost my color just as my work had earlier lost its spark.

I was aware that my midlife soul needed some reviving. The spark in me had grown faint. I was blowing softly on the embers as I took up writing and painting in the early 1990s. I was feeding the fire by resting for several months in 1995. It was the loss of my marriage that made me wake up, as the Buddhists would say, and seek the holy in new ways. I could no longer just go along and enjoy a spirituality of daily life when I felt I had no life at all.

I thought falling in love and getting married would save me from loneliness and unhappiness, just as I thought doing work I loved would save me from burnout. I had chosen to seek the holy in the practice of tending to a partnership. When that ceased to be an option, I had to look elsewhere.

In the months and years that followed, as I began to recover from the loss, I felt more and more that life's winding path was taking me back to the center of myself. I discovered that my own feelings were what I feared the most. Eventually I was even able to say that I was grateful for what had happened.

Relationships, work, art, and even writing are containers for the soup of life. They are not life itself. The labyrinth is a path, but life is in the walking. Each twist in the path made an opening for me to reconnect with myself and to learn something new. A good long break from my work reminded me to relax and play, renewing my sense of delight. Heartbreak taught me to come back to the center and to rest in God.

Life, like the labyrinth, is a long and winding path with twists and turns where if we are lucky we'll bump into ourselves. These days I try to go slowly, to feel my feelings, and to notice my life while it is happening. There is more of life to come.

Volume 24, Number 3, September 2003

COCOON

When I was a freshman in college, I had a bright pink poster on the wall of my fourth floor dorm room that I shared with Phyllis Hough. The poster had a line drawing of a butterfly on it and these words, "You can fly too, but that cocoon will have to go."

I think of this as the season of relinquishment. I was just telling the story recently of losing my Christmas sweater in 1989 and then losing my partner, my house, my town, and some of my friends all in the process of falling in love with that rascal John Ott and moving to Philadelphia.

Relinquishing the cocoon.

Relinquishing the labyrinth. This year in the fall my lovely forty-by-forty-foot canvas labyrinth got damaged. It had gotten some spots on it. The worst one was either tar or very dirty candle wax from the floor of Duke Chapel. So I took the labyrinth to a very reputable dry cleaner in Greensboro and asked them to work on the spots. They had done this for me several years before when the labyrinth got coffee on it.

I still don't know how it happened, but someone at the dry cleaners put two of the six-foot wide, forty-foot-long sections of the labyrinth in a washing machine and dryer. The purple painted lines that delineate the paths faded and ran around on the canvas so it now looks slightly marbleized. I might have been able to continue using it in a somewhat discolored state, but it also shrunk by about ten percent. This means that the paths no longer fit.

This experience with the labyrinth has made me wonder if there are big pieces of my life that don't fit. Judging from the level of exhaustion and my feeling of being overwhelmed, I'd say I have a bit too much crammed into my one life at the moment.

What do I do with my time? Why can't I get myself to sit quietly or to do a little yoga every day? Where does this feeling of being in such a rush all the time come from?

I've been asking this question of my friends and colleagues in recent weeks. And this is the answer we've come up with: mortality. We are going to die. This comes as no surprise to any of us, but in the spring and summer of the year some of us can delude ourselves into thinking we will go on growing and expanding and live forever. Then the days get short and the nights get cold. The trees lose their leaves and the world turns brown and we remember that we are finite.

My response seems to be to rush. To cram more in. And the activities of the season oblige. There are more events, more gatherings, more places to go, more things to do for other people, and lots of end-of-the-year work.

And the next thing I know, I'm out of whack.

Now about this butterfly, this creature of the air, this powerful metaphor for transformation. This butterfly that flies through the air with the greatest of ease, like the daring young woman on the flying....

I went to California for a friend's sixtieth birthday party. The party was held at Sam Keen's home. Sam has a full-size circus trapeze rig set up on his property in Sonoma, California, and has written a book about it, *Learning to Fly*. As part of the celebration, several of us flew on the trapeze.

The idea of swinging on a trapeze did not frighten me. I was a diver when I was young and I liked gymnastics. So I happily donned the safety belt and listened to a circus professional give instructions.

When it was my turn I climbed the narrow ladder up past the net and onto a small wooden platform twenty-four feet in the air. A nice woman hooked two ropes to my safety belt and hauled in the trapeze. As she hung onto the back of my belt, she said to grab the trapeze, lean out, and jump off the platform when she said, "Ready, hep." Sounds easy enough, but by this time I was scared out of my wits. My mind was racing, "Jump? Are you crazy? If I jump off this platform, the weight of my body will rip my arms right out of their sockets. I won't be able to hang on."

"Ready, hep," she said, just as she had promised. "Wait, wait," I said. "Ready, hep." "Could we talk about this?" "Ready, hep." Oh well, it was as good a day as any to be drawn and quartered. I jumped.

And then I soared through the air with the greatest of ease. The momentum was not down; it was forward. I was even breathing. The circus-trained professional on the ground holding the safety ropes said, "Knees up." At the far end of the arc of my swing the momentum allowed me to easily raise my knees and hook them over the bar. "Hands off." I let go and there I was swinging upside down by my knees.

I was in no danger at all. There was a huge net and if I had fallen the man with the ropes would have hung on and lowered me slowly to the net, as he did when he finally got me to hang by my hands again and let go and sit down in the net.

One lucky part of my personality is that I get myself into scary situations before I notice how scary they might be. I wasn't the slightest bit afraid of the trapeze until I was standing on the platform twenty-four feet in the air. And then I was so scared I thought I might pass out. Before I could clear my mind, I had jumped off the dang plank and was flying.

In this season the very things I need to let go of are things as common and familiar as the ground or planks under my feet. I take on too much. I offer to be in charge of too much. And to not do it scares me as much as jumping off a platform. To not do it means I have to face not doing, just being, and possibly my own finitude.

Volume 24, Number 4, December 2003

EVELYN

Sr. Evelyn Matter died on November 30 this year, the first Sunday of Advent. What an appropriate day, the first day of the Christian year, for her to go home to be with Jesus.

Evelyn Mattern graced my life with her presence for more than twenty-five years. She is all over my work, my faith, my writing, all over conversations about justice and spirituality, all over farmworkers and the death penalty. She was a tireless worker for justice. I once heard her say, "The price of freedom is constant vigilance."

Evelyn was a nun, but not the regular kind. She left her order after Vatican II and joined a new group called Sisters for Christian Community, a non-canonical order, meaning no pope or bishop was in charge of them.

Evelyn and I worked together, primarily on the North Carolina Council of Churches Committee for Equal Rights. She was the Council staff person assigned to the committee, which was formed during the Equal Rights Amendment campaign. When the amendment failed in North Carolina in 1982, the committee refused to disband. The meetings were so much fun that we used to say people would pay to attend them.

Evelyn, the Equal Rights Committee, and I planned many conferences together on women, faith, and public policy issues, such as economic justice, and violence against women. Evelyn left the Council of Churches in 1990, a little worn out from all the lobbying and committee work she did. The work felt much harder without her.

When she returned to the Council in 1996, many of the members of the Equal Rights Committee were turning eighty and not able to attend meetings as regularly. So Evelyn reshaped the group into a Task Force on the Impact of the Women's Movement on the Religious Community in North Carolina. One of her last completed projects was to compile the interviews the Task Force conducted into a readers theater, which she called The Woman's Coffeehouse of Spirit. The last time I saw her was at a production of the readers theater in May.

Evelyn, who held a PhD in English Literature from the University of Pennsylvania, was a writer and a poet. She wrote a book about the Beatitudes, *Blessed Are You: The Beatitudes and Our Survival*, and collaborated with an artist friend on a book of poetry and art, *Why Not Become the Fire? Encounters with Women Mystics*. She taught English in the prisons before I knew her. When she was away from the Council of Churches in the 1990s she taught English in North Carolina community colleges.

Justice and spirituality lived hand in hand in her life. She lived in a tiny log house, way out in the woods north of Raleigh, which she called Peace Hill. She had a sweet dog named Paz who predeceased her.

I always thought the dog's name was a play on words. When you said the name it sounded like paws, pause, and *paz*, the Latin for peace.

Hospitality was part of Evelyn's spiritual practice. She cared for so many of us. She loved us, led us, prayed for us. When groups met at her house, she fed us simple wholesome food. Whenever I doubted myself and mentioned it to Evelyn, she offered some word of encouragement. When I complained that editing my book of essays was taking too long, she said, "Writing just takes a long time."

When she knew there was nothing else to be done about her lung cancer, she sent word to all her friends that she was at peace. No one ever heard her ask, "Why me?"

Evelyn Mattern was greatly loved and admired. Over 250 people attended a farewell luncheon for her in September. Then she moved to Philadelphia, to the neighborhood where she grew up, to live her final days in a Catholic hospice.

One person who visited her in Philadelphia offered her the use of a cell phone. Evelyn said she had no use for one. She had gone home to learn to die and she was busy.

Evelyn was never far from God. You could feel the Holy in her house. You could see it in her face. She knew God in the midst of all of life, all the joys and all the sorrow. She once wrote me, "I guess the problem with Lent/dirt and ashes is that you don't know that Easter/daffodils are on the other side. You are in that unknowing period. It is your view, and nobody else can see it. We can only remind you that we are here and praying."

Now she views life from another side. From there, I feel certain, she prays for us every day.

The North Carolina Council of Churches held a memorial service for Sr. Evelyn Mattern on January 7 at the United Church of Chapel Hill. January 7 was Evelyn's birthday. She would have turned sixty-three.

Number 24, Number 4, December 2003

ANTIDOTE

an•ti•dote n : a remedy to counteract the effects of poison

I took the labyrinth to Asheville, North Carolina, in early March for a program sponsored by Holy Ground, a group similar to RCWMS. Fifty women came to walk, meditate, and pray. I suggested to the group that walking the labyrinth together could be an antidote to Mel Gibson's infamous movie *The Passion of the Christ* (now playing at a theater too near you.)

As I write, we are in the third week of Lent in the Christian calendar. It is mid-March. Daffodils splash color across my garden and tulip poplars bravely bloom around town. Each year we wait in suspense to see if their lovely blossoms will be withered by a late freeze.

A tiny piece of paper floats around on my desk bearing these words, "war, male violence, crucifixion, and resurrection." I think it is left from this time last year when we were all waiting to see if George Bush would invade Iraq. He did.

In a *Tikkun* magazine article on the war in Iraq, Richard Lowery quotes 2 Samuel 11:1–2, "In the spring of the year, when kings go to war…." Lowery comments, "The writer's deadpan assertion that spring is the time 'when kings go to war' may be a simple statement of fact. But it also underlines the distinctly unnatural character of a political system that generates death and destruction at precisely the time Nature calls forth new life and hope."

I feel that way about Easter every year. At the precise moment when the earth is bursting with life and color, when the ground is soft and fertile, the church asks me to return to winter, to the crucifixion and the tomb. It always feels like disavowing the cycles of the earth.

For years I've noticed that Holy Week and Easter are often out of sync with the weather. Holy Week, when we are supposed to be sad, can be bright and sunny, and then Easter can be cold and rainy. This used to be a minor irritation. It was no fun to wear a new Easter frock on a cold gray day. Then finally, it made me mad.

Winter is a natural time to contemplate loss and sacrifice. It is a time to go into the dark places in our own souls. Why not commemorate the death of God then? Why say, "Excuse me flowers, could you drop dead for a few days while we return to darkness?" Why not work in concert with the earth?

The story of Persephone spending the winter months in the underworld and then bringing spring with her when she returns to the surface of the earth makes more sense than the story about a male god who makes it all happen in three days. What is that? I fear that it is the same impulse as much of patriarchal religious tradition. It is an attempt to say that the way the natural world does it is not good enough. A mythic world created by men (and I mean men) is more blessed and glorious.

Take baptism for example. While I love the sacrament of baptism and the ritual reception of an infant into the faith community, it always bothers me the way baptism suggests that being born of a woman is not good enough. An infant has to be washed clean by the water of the church.

It's hard to be critical of Easter when you're a Presbyterian minister. Isn't Easter central to the Christian faith? Didn't Jesus die for my sins? Isn't that what I said I believed when I joined the church and again when I was ordained? You would think, but actually no.

Mel Gibson lost me completely when he said the point of Jesus' life was his death. Jesus' life was the point of his life. He was killed for his dangerous political message.

Welcome to the swamp known as atonement theory. Atone actually means to become reconciled or to return to harmony. We use the word today to mean, "to pay for" as in to be punished for. Traditional theology suggests that God was an angry parent who said, "Someone is going to pay for this!" Where did we get the idea that Jesus' death appeased an angry God?

Welcome to the realm of male violence. If God demands that kind of vengeful justice, then nations can demand it also. Why wouldn't the right wing in this country love a God who would exact excruciating suffering as payment for the sins of the world? An angry violent God lends sanction to wars of aggression.

Feminist theologians have spent decades untangling this problem. Atonement theory is well summarized in a pamphlet, *Christian Theology and Atonement Theory: Feminist Reflections,* by Shelley Wiley, published by RCWMS in 1995. It's way too complicated to explain in a few sentences, but you can read all about it in eighteen succinct pages.

I don't actually believe in a God who required a sacrifice in order to love humanity again. That seems pretty barbaric to me. I believe in a God who sent a precious prophet, the very child of God, to bring good news to the poor, release to the captive, and sight to the blind. Such a message was so dangerous to the Roman authorities and their local puppet government that Jesus was silenced. Jesus reconciled us to God by showing us that God loved us in spite of ourselves, not by dying but by living among us.

I like to think of Jesus as the antidote God sent to an ailing world. If Jesus came to the US today he'd tell us clean up the air, the water, and the soil, to rearrange the spending priorities in the federal budget, and to repent for creating more misery than good in the Middle East. I don't think Jesus would care which community of faith we belonged to so long as it brought good news to the poor, release to the captive, and sight to the blind.

God so loved the world that he sent Jesus, the prophets, and each one of us to help the world wake up. Jesus reminds me that I don't have to do anything to get God to love me. God just does it in spite of me. That's enough for me. I don't need buckets of blood to emphasize the point.

Volume 25, Number 1, March 2004

REPAIR

It is often easier to make something from scratch than to repair it later. Take the old house across the street from me, for example. It is being restored by a professional contractor, who intends to live in it but shakes his head and says, "Never again. This is too hard."

That's the feeling I had this fall when the labyrinth was damaged. Two of the seven panels that make up the forty-by-forty-foot floor cloth were accidentally washed and dried. The canvas shrunk by ten percent and the paint ran, creating a marbled effect. When I saw the damaged canvas for the first time, I started to cry.

A whole crew of us spent 180 hours making the labyrinth in 1997. It was hard work, but fun. I have a degree in mathematics and loved figuring out the geometry of the pattern. I practiced drawing it on small sheets of paper and finally on forty by forty feet of rolled-out newsprint. It was a great adventure, but not one I planned to repeat.

My marriage ended while we were making the labyrinth the first time. The canvas caught my tears. Its paths held me as I wandered, feeling lost and disoriented. Eventually it felt my dancing feet, as healing brought playful energy back into my life. Over the years it has welcomed the feet of thousands of pilgrims.

I held the ruined labyrinth panels in my hands this fall, conflicted about whether I wanted to hug it to my chest or throw it on the ground. I tried comforting myself with, "It's only a thing. It is not a person. No one has died." But my heart was broken all the same. I tried to push the feelings away with, "Oh, who cares? I was tired of hauling that thing around anyway."

Sometimes it is really hard to hold what is. It was hard to face the fact of a broken marriage and not say, "Oh well, it wasn't perfect anyway." It was hard to see the damaged labyrinth and not try to push it away from my heart when I felt overwhelmed and defeated. The prospect of making or even buying a whole new canvas seemed impossible. I didn't know whether to scream, sue someone, or give up.

When we tried to put the damaged labyrinth together, the full-size panels had to be gathered like draperies to fit the shrunken ones. The poor thing looked as ridiculous as a household cat dressed up in baby clothes. All I could do at that point was laugh.

I didn't know what else to do, so I did nothing at all for a while. I tried not to focus on my outrage, waiting for the feelings to settle and my head to clear. Finally, just before Christmas, I took the first steps towards repair.

I purchased eighty feet of canvas from my favorite art store in Raleigh. It took four of us to unroll the six-foot-wide canvas from a bolt in the art store's crowded back room. I found Velcro for sale online at a good price. Velcro connects the panels. I picked up a gallon of the same purple house paint we used six years before, along with some spongy brushes and rolls of masking tape. Taping the edges before painting makes clean lines. Having collected the supplies, I lined up a huge multipurpose room at a local church and invited friends to help remake the labyrinth on the last Friday of January.

Then it snowed.

It was not a big snow, just two or three inches. But then it rained and ice formed on top of the snow. School was cancelled. The side streets were like frozen ponds. Whatever thawed during the daytime froze solid again at night. I hiked the half-mile back and forth to my office to sew the Velcro onto the canvas.

Then my sewing machine broke.

Having a damaged labyrinth was challenging enough. Negotiating icy sidewalks to get to my office was another challenge. But having the sewing machine break was more than I could stand. My thirty-year-old Elna sewing machine with entirely metal parts had never let me down. It sewed the whole labyrinth the first time. Now, after just one panel, it had given out. That's when I lost it. "I can't do it. I can't fix it. This project is too big for me." I left the office and trudged home, feeling discouraged, disheartened, and defeated again.

I'm a sturdy person, with a good strong outer layer, like ice on top of snow. I usually have a sense of direction and an opinion on most issues. I can carry my share of emotional weight. I've survived two divorces (my parents' and my own) and my father's early death. I've learned that being sturdy isn't always the best approach. Sometimes yielding is what is called for. When I heard myself say, "I can't do it. I can't fix it," I said, "That's right. You can't fix it right now. Go home and rest."

When the sewing machine broke, the surface cracked and I could feel the messy feelings underneath. I felt vulnerable. I didn't know what was wrong. I couldn't fix it by myself. Maybe trying to repair a great big heavy canvas labyrinth, in the snow, by myself, was too hard. I don't like those messy feelings. I'd rather be cheerful and feel more or less in control of my life. It was only a broken sewing machine, after all. It was only a messed-up piece of cloth.

The next day I took the machine apart and saw that the main gear was stripped. I felt so much better. I knew what to do about that—take it to the sewing machine repair guy. But because of the snow, he was backed up, so I had to find another machine. I felt better just having a plan.

I remembered there was a woman down the street who used to own a sewing business and still had some commercial machines. When I called, she offered to let me bring the canvas over and to finish sewing the Velcro on for me. Picture me carrying twenty-five pounds of canvas down an icy street. I only fell once, on my knees on top of the canvas, right in front of the Baptist church.

After that, I thought redrawing the pattern and painting the lines would be fun. I forgot that it is easier to make something from scratch than to repair it. The labyrinth is a circular pattern. When we laid the labyrinth out with the two new blank panels in it and tried to match up the circles, we couldn't make it work. It seems that our circles were not perfectly round.

It took one long day, twelve people, sixty hours, and finally it took Dwight and Meredith, the architectural designer and the engineer, to fill in the pattern. Did I mention that this was all done squatting on the floor? There were some very stiff muscles the next day.

When we laid it out in Duke Chapel on February 13, it looked beautiful. The hard work had paid off. After my friend B.J. walked the labyrinth I asked her if she noticed anything different. "I didn't remember that there were gaps in the lines before." "There are no gaps in the pattern. Show me," I said with surprise. Sure enough, there were three-foot gaps in some of the lines. I had been watching people walk all day and they seemed to be doing fine. That evening I filled in the pattern and realized the mistakes had been symmetrical, allowing people to walk the pattern in a slightly different way.

Six years ago remaking a damaged labyrinth was unthinkable, but then life never goes exactly as we plan. Hardly anything is ever really finished. Things change. That's all we know for sure. Perhaps we should stop being so surprised when they do.

Volume 25, Number 1, March 2004

WESTWARD

I've had great adventures this summer, and it is only the Fourth of July. The first and longest one was a trip to Oklahoma for my birthday in late May.

I'm big on birthdays. When I was small, my mother helped me plan birthday parties every year. Now I always try to do something special for my birthday. When I turned fifty, I went to Italy for two weeks and then threw myself a rock-and-roll dance party in a gym. (Please don't fail to celebrate your fiftieth birthday. People will do almost anything you ask them to, even dance.)

This year I kept feeling like I wanted to go to Oklahoma to see my mother for my birthday. Since her birthday is the day before mine, I could be in Tulsa for both of ours. She was turning eighty-two and I was turning fifty-three this year.

Since it is 1,100 miles from Durham, North Carolina, to Tulsa, I usually fly. But I just couldn't persuade myself to make plane reservations. I have a fear of flying that comes and goes. I say I'm willing to fly for things I'm willing to die for, which includes Italy, friends, and my mother. Ever since 9/11 it has been even harder to get myself to fly. Airports have become such inhospitable places.

A week before my birthday, I still did not have a travel plan, but I had an idea I might drive. I have a reliable car with air conditioning. (I'm too much of a wimp to drive across the South without it.) I wasn't even sure I could drive that far. The last time I made the trip, I was under twenty-five. "I can't drive all the way to Oklahoma by myself," I'd think. Then I'd say, "My office mate Mary-Russell rode her bicycle all the way from Durham to California, what do you mean you can't drive a perfectly good car to Oklahoma?" Mary-Russell says it is not possible to ride a bike from Durham to California, but you can ride a bike from

Durham to Greensboro, North Carolina, and then from Greensboro to the next place down the road.

So I decided to act as though I might actually do it and took the appropriate steps. I got a haircut, acquired road maps, and had the oil changed in my car. On Saturday I spent all morning packing and then got in my car and drove to Asheville, which I have done many times. I knew that if I refused to go any further, no harm would be done and I'd be in Asheville, which I like. I stopped on the way for my favorite walk around a small lake in Black Mountain and arrived at my friend Lucy's house at dark.

I bounced out of bed at 7:30 a.m. Sunday morning and headed across the mountains to Knoxville, stopping in Norris, Tennessee, a small town built by the TVA. (You remember the Tennessee Valley Authority.) North Carolina friends live in this sweet planned community with lots of green spaces. Then it was on across what must be the longest state east of the Mississippi, all the way to Memphis. I wandered the path beside the river, admired the trolley cars, saw the ducks in the fountain in the lobby of the Peabody Hotel, and spent the night.

On Monday I crossed the mighty Mississippi and the landscape changed dramatically. Rolling countryside gave way to flat rice fields, gorgeous sweeping rows of green. I had never imagined Basmati rice growing in Arkansas. I continued across Arkansas to Little Rock and the familiar Ozarks began. I spent seven summers of my young life at a camp in the northern Ozarks.

When I finally crossed the state line into Oklahoma, I got such a rush. It was so beautiful. You may have the wrong image of Oklahoma in your mind. Eastern Oklahoma and Tulsa are in the foothills of the Ozarks and are called "Green Country," because of all the rivers that have been dammed up to make lakes. Take that flat picture you get in your mind when I say Oklahoma, rumple it up, paint it green, and sprinkle around a few small oak trees. There you go.

Gently rolling open pastures with light green grasses and wildflowers blowing gently in the breeze. There was lots of space. I felt closer to the sky than I do in North Carolina where the trees are so much taller and closer together. I could imagine having been a Sooner in the Oklahoma land rush, sneaking in early to try to get a piece of that land; it was so lovely. It felt right. It looked like home.

Sometimes I have to shake myself to remember that I actually grew up in Oklahoma, it seems like so many years and so many miles away. I left eastern Oklahoma thirty-five years ago when I went off to college in New England, and I've never really lived there since. But I'm from there. And driving all that way helped me to know, once again, where there is. It is in the West. Once you cross the great mother river of the continent, you are in the West. And it is different. There is a little more space for the wild, for the untamed, perhaps for the imagination. The tornado sirens that went off while I was in Tulsa are only one example.

I went to Tulsa to see my mother. But I drove to Tulsa in order to see all the land between here and there. In the process, I was reminded that all the miles and all the years in between are, in fact, connected.

Volume 25, Number 2, July 2004

FEAR

The events of the last four years have been unnerving. In case you have trouble remembering your own life, as I do, let me review.

First we had the 2000 presidential election, which was the biggest mess I can remember. The outcome was unclear. We were confused for weeks. The Supreme Court eventually stopped the counting of disputed ballots in Florida, making George W. Bush the winner. The media, however, had all but decided the race on election night.

In *OutFoxed*, the MoveOn.org-sponsored documentary about Fox News, we learn that on election night, at about 2:00 a.m., Fox News called the election for Bush, with no justification whatsoever. The numbers coming out of Florida were still unclear. No winner had emerged, but within fifteen minutes all three of the major television networks followed suit. That set George Bush up as the apparent winner and Al Gore as the disgruntled challenger. The person in charge of the Fox newsroom on election night was Bush's cousin.

Nine months after the 2000 election came the horrific events of September 11. I'm cynical enough to have thought, "Watch out, the administration will use this to their own advantage." Before any of us could absorb the tragedy and loss, the White House was interpreting our grief and pushing their agenda forward. Instead of using the moment, our grief, and the world's sympathy to bring the American people together or improve relationships among nations, the US government moved to grab power, scare people at home, wage war abroad, and make the world safer for US oil interests.

Within a week Congress had passed President Bush's war resolution. Only Barbara Lee, the congresswoman from Oakland, California, voted against the measure giving the president the authority to do whatever he wanted to. The rest of Congress went along like sheep. All of them.

Using 9/11 as justification, Washington invaded Afghanistan, whittled away at our civil rights by passing the Patriot Act, and eventually invaded Iraq. The latter has cost us two hundred million dollars, a thousand American lives, and countless Iraqi lives.

From the beginning it has been hard to get reliable news about the Iraqi war. Keith Kay, a distinguished cameraman and producer who has covered several wars for major networks, decided not to even try. He told NPR that he'd rather stay home than put up with "press pools" and "embedded" journalists. "What happened to independent journalists independently observing the war?" he asked. Senior officers in Iraq, who were junior officers in Viet Nam, blame the press for the way that war turned out, according to Kay. I started reading an Irish journalist who writes for a British newspaper to get a clearer view of what the US was up to.

In *Fahrenheit 9/11*, Michael Moore made clear that one of the things the White House is up to is scaring the American public. Moore interviewed James McDermott, a US Congressman and a psychiatrist.

> Moore: Fear works.

> McDermott: Fear does work. Yes. You can make people do anything if they're afraid.

> Moore: And how do you make them afraid?

> McDermott: You make them afraid by creating an aura of endless threat. They [the administration] play this like an organ. They raise it up to orange, then up to red, then they dropped it back to orange, they gave these mixed messages, which were crazy-making.

The politics of fear continue. One outrageous example being Vice President Cheney's suggestion in early September that if we make the wrong choice in the November election, "then the danger is that we'll get hit again and we'll be hit in a way that will be devastating from the standpoint of the United States."

Fear can be a successful marketing strategy. Madison Avenue uses it all the time. Take hormone replacement therapy as an example. The drug companies and medical establishment convinced hundreds of thousands of women that if they didn't take drugs they would grow old, dry out, break their hips, get heart disease, and lose their libido. The implied message was that women would become unlovable, hunched-over old hags who would be left alone to die a painful death.

I refuse to give in to the forces of darkness or to think of the world as an evil place. Of course lots of people in other countries hate us. After what the United States has done in the last few years they have every reason to. It is our job to stop being the bullies.

I refuse to be discouraged. It has been years since I have seen such a groundswell of interest in an election. I know people who are throwing parties to raise money for their candidates. I have one young friend who stayed out of college for a semester to work for hers. Some of the media are trying to tell us that the election is already over. It's not.

Our job is to stop responding to the politics of fear. Our job is to talk with our friends and neighbors about the issues in the election, and I don't mean whether John Kerry deserved his war medals. We need to be talking about the cost of the war in Iraq, the destruction of the environment, the expense of health care, the erosion of public education, and our role as citizens of the world. As Michael Moore suggested in an e-mail in late September, we need to stop wringing our hands and take a voter to the polls.

Volume 25, Number 3, October 2004

SABBATH TIME

I passed the neighborhood rabbi on a cloudy Saturday afternoon early this fall. He was strolling, umbrella in hand, his wife and another woman by his side. I sped past in my car. "It's the Sabbath," I thought, remembering the prohibition against work on the Sabbath (which includes driving unless it is absolutely necessary). "Sabbath time," I thought. "How badly we all need it."

I arranged a break for myself in late August this year and spent ten days at the North Carolina coast. I needed to get away from my speeding life and from all the things that demand my attention when I'm at home. I was becoming a very grumpy person.

I stayed at Pelican House, the retreat house on the beach at Trinity Center. For ten days, I didn't drive a car or answer a phone and hardly made a decision. I ate the conference center's food, walked on the beach, wrote, and painted. It was delicious and long enough to actually get bored.

This extended break at the beach reminded me of long stretches of time I had in California several years ago. My then-husband had so much work in San Francisco in 1996 and 1997 that we decided to rent a place.

In January of 1997 we located a lovely apartment through a friend of a friend. It was such a sweet space, decorated in attractive monotones, and located in the lower level of a house way up in Diamond Heights, a neighborhood near Twin Peaks.

Four windows faced north and east out of the living room, providing a spectacular view of the city and the bay below. I especially liked the view out of the smallest of the four, from which I could see the top of a pine tree in the neighbor's yard, a spit of water by the Bay Bridge, and the Oakland hills beyond.

One morning I sat on the off-white sofa and watched the sun rise over the top of the hills turning the world sundry shades of pink. First the tops of the Oakland hills turned rosy along with the clouds above them. As the sun crested the peaks it bathed the hills in blazing light turning them white and edging the clouds golden. Blinding light, like a thousand candles, made specks before my eyes. The white walls of the living room were awash in the bright yellow light of dawn.

There was a terraced garden behind the apartment where the landlord grew flowers and a few vegetables. Two artichokes grew at the end of straight stalks like little pineapples. The house was on such a steep San Francisco hill that if the backyard had not been terraced, an artichoke dropped near the house would have rolled straight down to the street below. I remember one late morning when I stepped out into the garden and found the warm air filled with small white butterflies landing first on tiny white irises and then on the pink flowers that sprang open in the ground cover each day.

I had been quite happy to sit and write at the Danish modern table I used for a desk. I can remember feeling satisfied that I was doing just what I was supposed to do. In San Francisco I had time to write, to muse, to collect ideas in the basket of my mind and let them roll around together. I had grown fond of the gentle oscillation of my life between North Carolina and California. At home in Durham, there were retreats to plan, a house to run, a garden to tend, and a phone that rang constantly with both enticing and irritating requests. When I made the trip to San Francisco every few months, and stayed for a couple of weeks, it was like being on retreat. I wrote more because I had so much more uninterrupted time. I wandered the city by myself and got lost in my own thoughts.

Though California was enchanting, I never wanted to live there fulltime. I prefer walking on flatter ground in a smaller town. I like the change of seasons and the easy way people form connections in North Carolina.

I lost my San Francisco retreat when my husband and I separated in September 1997 and he moved there permanently. I must have taken the sweet memories of my time in California and hidden them someplace dark and safe. It was only while I was at the beach in August this year that I got interested in them and went looking for them in my journals. There I found descriptions of the light, the garden, and the restful days. It has taken seven years of healing for me to want to get these sweet memories out again.

The days of resting at the beach this summer reminded me of my time in San Francisco. It had been a treat to have a home away from home, a place of quiet and contemplation. I noticed this summer that I am once again beginning to have such a place. I lead so many programs at Trinity Center that it has become comfortably familiar and is now my favorite place to write. There is one particular room with a view of the ocean where I am almost always able to relax and concentrate. It is becoming a place where I can slow, a place where I can have Sabbath time.

Volume 25, Number 3, October 2004

NANCY

The following are my edited remarks for two memorial services for Nancy Peeler Keppel, one in Blacksburg, Virginia, December 14, 2004, and one at Nancy's home church, Community United Church of Christ, Raleigh, North Carolina, January 22, 2005.

We are gathered here today to celebrate the life and grieve the loss of our mother, sister, friend, and best cheerleader, Nancy Peeler Keppel.

St. John Chrysostom says, "Know that she whom we love and lose is no longer where she was before. She is now wherever we are."

I met Nancy in 1980 when Carol Bernard Snyder arranged for us to share a room at a national United Church of Christ (UCC) women's meeting. The first time I laid eyes on her was at the Greensboro airport as we all prepared to fly off to the meeting. I was almost thirty; she was fifty. I wondered who this short, outspoken, unusual older woman was.

In the 1980s, Nancy and I served together on the North Carolina Council of Churches Committee for the Equal Rights Amendment. She had been instrumental in the formation of the Task Force for Women in Church and Society of the Southern Conference of the UCC. She served on the Board of the Resource Center for Women and Ministry in the South. I came to love Nancy like a sister and struggle with her as a friend. She would go on and on about people I did not know and I'd have to stop her and say, "Slow down. Whom are you talking about?"

In the last couple of years, Nancy and I edited a book together, a collection of essays by UCC clergywomen called *God Speaks, Women Respond*. We talked on the phone every few days. I came to know Nancy's deep faith in God as we struggled with publishers and as she weathered her cancer treatments with grace and humor. She heard God's call and saw God's hand everywhere in her life. She was a tireless worker for justice for women, for gay and lesbian people, for the poor, and for the world. She was sturdy. Until the very end, she never lost her appetite or ability to sleep or interest in Duke basketball. When her doctor told her that cancer patients who fell in love and ate chocolate got along better, she said she'd be happy to oblige.

Nancy made things happen in the world by pushing. She would call me up and tell me what to do. I'd take a deep breath and usually do it. I would not call her critical, but she had an idea about how to improve almost anything. The only argument I ever won with her was over the color of the cover of our book. She wanted it to be red and stand out! I wanted it to be blue and pretty. When she gave in, I was stunned. I will never know how she came to the decision. I took it as a gift she gave me.

The numbers of people who were touched by Nancy are legion. I spoke to one, Mary Emma Evans, shortly after Nancy died. Mary Emma is a pastor and gospel singer in North Carolina whom Nancy helped write a chapter for the book and also helped to produce a musical CD. Mary Emma was singing "Beulah Land" at the top of her lungs to an audience of several hundred people in North Carolina at the moment Nancy died. She said a spirit filled that hall like she had never felt before. Mary Emma said, "Nancy helped me so much. She couldn't have encouraged and supported anyone more than me." The truth is that there are scores of people like Mary Emma around the country whom Nancy enabled to be and do more than they thought they could.

Nancy gave her energy, her love, and her insistent encouragement to her projects, to her beloved United Church of Christ, and to her family. Her children Tim, Ken, and Jane were her finest accomplishment. She loved them. She tried to boss them around. She was so proud of them. She talked about them to anyone who would listen. She was so amazed by them.

Her grandchildren were her great joy. These girls and boys were the sweetest gifts in her life. Oh, how she loved to see them! What more could any human being ask than to be surrounded at the moment of death by children, grandchildren, and friends. What more could any person ask than to be remembered by such people.

The poet Khalil Gibran has written,

> Close your eyes and you will see me among you now and always. Go back to your homes and you will find there what death could not take away from you and from me.

Nancy told her daughter Jane that she, Nancy, would be watching her. Nancy's energy is still with us, asking questions, being impatient, pushing us along, making us better than we thought we could be.

In "When Death Comes," Mary Oliver has written:

> When death comes....
> When it's over, I don't want to wonder
> if I have made of my life something particular, and real....
> I don't want to end up simply having visited this world.

Nancy Peeler Keppel did more than just visit this world. She lived her life in amazement and wonder, grateful to God for each and every day of it until the last.

For the sweet blessing of Nancy's presence among us, for the gracious God who created her and now holds her in loving arms, and for each person here, we give thanks and praise. Amen.

Volume 25 Number 4, January 2005

WINTER

I spent Christmas Eve at my local church in Chapel Hill. As I sat down on one of the new red upholstered chairs, I greeted the woman next to me and mentioned having just seen her lovely grown daughter. "I wish I had," she responded. Oh, right—divided families. The daughter was visiting her father in Durham. The mom lives in Chapel Hill.

As we sang carols, I thought of the divided places in my own life and felt sad. No, more than sad, gypped. Why couldn't we have peace on earth and peace in our homes just one Christmas? It had been a pretty rough fall.

The election in November had been disheartening and had left ongoing questions about election fraud, lost ballots, and questionable voting machines. Ahead of us are four more years of an administration that seems determined to continue an unjust war, whittle away at the Bill of Rights, further erode reproductive rights, appoint right-wing activist judges, open forests everywhere to logging, drill for oil in the Arctic wildlife refuge, gut the few remaining social programs, and dismantle Social Security. I was feeling pretty glum.

On December 1, I learned that CBS and NBC networks had refused to run a thirty-second television ad from the United Church of Christ because its all-inclusive welcome was deemed "too controversial." It made me so mad that I called the UCC press contact for details, called the local TV network affiliates, and e-mailed everyone I could think of. The ad showed people being turned away from the church, some of whom might have been gay or lesbian couples.

"Because this commercial touches on the exclusion of gay couples and other minority groups by other individuals and organizations," reads an explanation from CBS, "and the fact the Executive Branch has recently proposed a Constitutional Amendment to define marriage as a union between a man and a woman, this spot is unacceptable for broadcast on the [CBS and UPN] networks."

The ad said nothing about same-sex marriage. I concluded that the major networks were either scared by or under the control of the current administration and that the administration's agenda would repeatedly influence network policy.

As it turned out, the UCC received more publicity from the controversy than they ever would have from the ad campaign. National UCC figures were heard and seen on TV, radio, newspapers, and magazines. Some UCC congregations reported an increase in calls and visitors.

The controversy over the UCC ad sounded like another controversy closer to home. In October, WUNC, a public radio station in Chapel Hill, refused to run an underwriting announcement from Ipas, an international reproductive health organization. WUNC had run the announcement earlier in the year but decided the word "rights" constituted advocacy, which violated guidelines for these sponsor slots.

The ad stated, "Ipas, a Chapel Hill-based nonprofit that protects women's reproductive health and rights at home and abroad. More information available at www.ipas.org." Ipas would not take out the word "rights" and pulled its underwriting support.

So now we can't say "reproductive rights" out loud? Sex education, family planning, and good gynecological care are all part of reproductive rights.

On December 2, the Rev. Beth Stroud was defrocked by The United Methodist Church. The lesbian clergywoman in Pennsylvania was found guilty of "engaging in practices that are incompatible with Christian teachings." The motto of the United Methodisth Church is "Open hearts. Open minds. Open doors." One might ask, "Open to whom?"

Then in early December, I learned that my friend and colleague Nancy Peeler Keppel was nearing the end of her life. Nancy had helped to fund our writing programs over the last three years. She and I had edited a book together that was published in 2004. She was a remarkable woman and you can read more about her elsewhere in this newsletter. I made one last visit to Nancy on December 10, and she died on December 12.

Compared with the fall, I thought the winter holidays, even with all their activity, were going to be a welcome break, and they were for me personally. I enjoyed writing every morning but Christmas and New Year's Day. But on the morning after Christmas, we all woke to the news that southern Asia had been devastated by an earthquake under the Indian Ocean and a tsunami that had killed thousands. As the weeks have passed the death toll has risen above 150,000. Religious organizations, governments, and aid organizations around the world have sent money, supplies, and workers to help in the aftermath.

A right-wing administration in Washington, the rights of LGBT people being challenged in the church and in the media, a natural disaster of staggering proportions. It was a lot to hold.

As I sat in my red chair on Christmas Eve, I considered the difficult fall. (The tsunami was yet to come.) I held a lighted candle before me and began to wonder. What better place to bring my own sadness and the brokenness of the world than to a God who would consider appearing in the world as a helpless child? Perhaps such a child, or his mother, could hold all that is not right with the world. What better place to take our brokenness than to a community of people who would pause for a moment at the darkest time of the year and announce the return of the light. What? I had thought life would be simple, easy, without complications? No. This is the life we are given, with its joys and sorrows that come all at once. This is the life we are fortunate enough to live.

Volume 25, Number 4, January 2005

BUDDHIST

I saw an ad for a conference on women and Buddhism to be held at Smith College in April, and I immediately thought of Rachael. It would be an excuse to visit my alma mater and a nice spring outing. Though not a practicing Buddhist, I am interested in feminist perspectives on religion, any religion. Rachael, however, is a Tibetan Buddhist dharma teacher. I thought she needed to go and it would be fun to go along.

I first encountered Buddhism when I visited Japan at age ten. Later, in college, I took a class on Zen Buddhism from Taitetsu Unno. As part of the course, Prof. Unno organized a sesshin, a weekend of sitting led by a Japanese roshi or teacher. The roshi told us not to take notes on his talks. "Anything I say that is important to you will go inside of you and live there." Mostly what I remember from the weekend is sitting still for endless hours while staring at a crack in the floor. I didn't think I ever needed to try that again, and it was another twenty years before I wanted to try meditation of any kind. But I loved learning that I did not always have to take notes.

Rachael and I traveled to Northampton with two other women from her meditation group in Raleigh, North Carolina. They all stayed in a bed and breakfast while I stayed with Adrienne, an eighty-three-year-old friend from my hometown, who spent her adult life teaching music at Smith. On the first morning of the conference, my traveling companions picked me up at Adrienne's and took me the short distance to the college chapel for the program.

The college's pleasantly plain, white, New England-style chapel was filled with women and a few men. I noticed a number of women with shaved heads and either red or black robes. As one of the speakers said, "Women and Buddhism" can include nuns, priests, practitioners, and people with a bedside book on Buddhism. We had them all. During the conference, I attended talks and panels on women in Buddhism, engaged Buddhism, and women changing Buddhism. There was a lecture by bell hooks, a reading by poet Jane Hirschfield and a performance by musical artist Meredith Monk, but wandering around the campus was the thing I enjoyed the most. I explored the steamy tropical Victorian greenhouses, strolled by Paradise Pond, and took a couple of walks through the wooded area beside the Mill River. It was an unusually warm weekend for Massachusetts in April, and being outside was meditation practice enough for me.

In the afternoon, I attended a Japanese tea ceremony led by Alice Unno, the wife of my Zen professor. As a young married woman, she had lived in Japan and studied the tea ceremony while Prof. Unno studied religion. Alice is a small, tidy woman, well practiced in the precise movements of the ceremony. As she poured water from a wooden ladle, set it down with care, and then whipped the tea into a greenish froth, I recalled her making the same motions more than thirty years before. At the end of the ceremony, I thanked her for sharing her practice with me once again.

As I left the classroom building where the ceremony was held, I remembered walking out of that same building with Alice Unno many years before just as it had begun to snow. "Oh, no," one student had exclaimed, "I have to drive to Boston. This is terrible." "Hurrah," cheered another, "perhaps my test will be called off tomorrow." Alice Unno gazed out at the snow and said quietly, "It's snowing." Later I learned that seeing things as they are is one aim of Buddhist practice. I never needed a better example than Alice Unno in the snow.

The conference planners failed to see one issue as it really is today. They somehow overlooked sexual misconduct as a topic for the program. Since the misconduct of leaders in Buddhist communities has been in the news, it seems clear that Buddhists, like every other religious group, need to deal with the issue. Though not on the program, the topic came up in the question and answer periods. I nearly jumped out of my seat when I heard someone ask a question about whether it was "right speech" to speak badly of any teacher.

This is not a new topic. Protestant, Catholic, and Jewish communities have been working on issues of sexual misconduct among professionals in their communities for thirty years, aided by the work of Marie Fortune, Mary Pellauer, Carol Adams, and others. I realized that the American Buddhist community is still young. Many of the western women who became Buddhists left their former faiths years ago and may have missed the work on misconduct in other faith communities. One would think that at least the Buddhist academics would be up to speed on the issue, as colleges and universities have had to deal with the issue. One can find research, guidelines, and procedures to apply to any faith.

As I see it, students have a right to fall in love with their teachers, clients with their therapists, parishioners and members with their ministers, rabbis, or priests. It is the responsibility of the professional to hold the line and it is the responsibility of the supervising profession, organization, or religion to see to it that they do.

Why should I expect the Buddhist community to be any more advanced in dealing with difficult issues than any other community? Buddhism, for all its considerable wisdom, grew out of patriarchal societies in which the treatment of women was not great.

At the end of the conference, one of the organizers apologized; she had not realized that misconduct was such a big issue. The various branches of Buddhism in the west will grow as women share their visions and insights. And we will all grow as Buddhism helps us to walk mindfully and to see things as they really are.

Volume 26, Number 2, July 2005

DIVING

When I was in Tulsa, Oklahoma, this summer, I went swimming with my niece Lily, not quite five. A competent only child, Lily directed our play in the water. "Catch me when I go down the slide," she instructed as she climbed the bright blue and yellow plastic children's slide. After a few times down the slide, she said she did not need me anymore and could do it on her own. I watched her splash into the water and then swim like a fish to the side, get out and do it again. When she tired of the slide, I asked if she wanted to watch me jump off the diving board. She agreed and we left the children's area for the thirteen-foot deep diving tank with two low boards and a high one. After I took three long strides down the board, bounced once on the end, and jumped in, remembering to point my toes and stay straight as a stick, it was "Catch me when I jump off the board, Aunt Jeanette." I positioned myself near the spot where she might enter the water and told her to try not to jump right on me. Two jumps later, she was saying, "I can do it by myself." I watched for a while, as did a lifeguard, and then took up jumping or doing a simple dive off one board while Lily jumped off the other.

Finally I got up my nerve to climb the ladder to the high diving board. It felt like it was twenty feet in the air, though I doubt it was over twelve. I inched my way out to the end of the board and tried to blank out the idea of falling off sideways and killing myself. I stood calmly, took a deep breath, and stepped off into space. My only thought was, "Stay real straight or this could hurt." The next thing I knew I was swimming like crazy through a mass of bubbles, reaching for the surface and air. Even straight as a stick, I hit the water hard and wondered about the wisdom of such antics at age fifty-four. Lily said that next year she's going to try the high board and I allowed as how I thought that was a good idea.

It is hard to believe that at summer camp just forty years ago, I was able to do an inverted somersault off the high diving board. That's the one where you run out to the end of the diving board, throw yourself up into the air, flip over backwards towards the board making sure not to hit your head on it, spin around one and half times, and dive in the water head first. (I think the summer camp still has it on 16mm movie film if you want to see it.) As a scared adult, I now wonder how I, a small, finicky, well-protected child, was ever able to learn to do such tricks. I remember receiving good instruction from a great coach, learning each dive incrementally, and wearing a sweatshirt in case I landed splat on my back, but still it seems totally impossible to me now.

When I was recently with my cousin Beth (my father's brother's daughter), she reminded me that our grandfather, Henry Stokes, could walk on his hands. I did not know him well. He was already old, maybe sixty, when I was born in Oklahoma, and he lived in Georgia, so he never walked on his hands for me. He also gambled and lied about it to Viola, my rigid Southern Baptist grandmother, which I always liked about him.

I never realized I was descended from circus people until Beth and I were talking. Henry worked for the circus when he was young, perhaps walking on his hands. I already knew Viola's father had owned a whirly gig and must have traveled with the circus, but it surprised me to learn that my grandfather had circus connections as well.

My father, Malcolm Stokes, inherited his father's coordination and put it to use in the water. Daddy was a fancy diver for the Duke University swim team, the Mermen, from 1934–36. He also did exhibition diving at the Hotel De Soto, a fancy downtown hotel in his hometown of Savannah, Georgia. Mother says he worked as a lifeguard at the beach in the summers to make money. I don't know Savannah well. I remember little from a visit when I was four, and when I was there in my thirties, it poured rain the whole time. I had to look at a map to remind myself that Savannah is on a river that empties into the ocean, and I had to ask a native to learn that the beach at Tybee Island is only eighteen miles away.

When my parents moved to Tulsa in the 1940s for my father's medical practice, Daddy joined a club with a swimming pool and a golf course.

He and a family friend taught me to swim and dive. My Texas mother eventually made herself learn to swim just well enough to pluck me from the deep end should I flounder. When I was eight, my parents built a house with a swimming pool. My father made sure it was a heated swimming pool, so he could dive in the water first thing in the morning. I can still picture my father sliding open the glass door of his bedroom, taking two steps across the covered porch, stepping off the porch, and diving in the water. Now that I think of it, it is one of my strongest images of my father, suspended in the air, arms and body outstretched, reaching headfirst for the water.

I knew, of course, that my father could swim and dive, but had never given it much thought. He had so many talents, as a doctor, a surgeon, an amateur golfer, and a musician. I never really stopped to think about his connection to the water until recently. He has been dead for nearly thirty years and wanders in and out of my consciousness rather unpredictably. I've noticed that in the last couple of years I have oriented my life towards the ocean. I've managed to plan so many work-related events at a conference center on the North Carolina coast that in 2004 I spent twenty-eight days by the sea. While swimming in the ocean on one of those days last year, it struck me, perhaps for the first time, that my father loved the ocean. I could remember being in it with him several times. It feels like stating the obvious, but he was a man who grew up next to the Atlantic Ocean and who spent his whole adult life landlocked in Oklahoma.

Sitting by the swimming pool in the scorching Oklahoma heat this summer, watching my energetic niece jump into the water again and again, I realized that my ancestors had made it easier for me to overcome my fear and do somersaults off the high board. My father was a fancy diver with saltwater in his veins and my grandfather could walk on his hands.

Volume 26, Number 2, July 2005

GODDESSES

I was a raving lunatic for the first two weeks of November. A combination of things happened on Halloween that sent me over the edge. That morning's e-mail brought news that President Bush had nominated another right-wing judge to the Supreme Court and the sad news that Christine, the wife of a colleague in Florida, had died of a brain tumor. The president's slap in the face to feminists and the loss of one fine woman rocked me at a deep level. Something snapped inside of me and a voice started screaming, "That's it! I have to do something to stop the madness."

I started e-mailing money to good causes and messages to the president and Congress—to stop the war, the torture, the tax cuts, the attempts to drill in the Arctic National Wildlife Preserve, and the right-wing judicial appointments. I also wrote the governor of North Carolina asking him to stop the executions. There were three scheduled this fall and all three took place. I kept at this insistent communicating every day for two weeks.

As I calmed down, I returned to my current spiritual practice of trying to get myself to e-mail or write at least one elected official each week. As Sr. Evelyn Mattern once said, "The price of freedom is constant vigilance."

Meanwhile, I felt Christine's death and her family's grief more intensely than I had anticipated. I hardly knew her. I had only met her once, but I had developed a deep concern for her as I followed her yearlong illness from afar. I was grateful that her husband Tom, a Presbyterian minister, decided to have two memorial services, one in Florida where they lived and a second in Durham where they had many friends and family.

I attended the service in Durham and was especially touched by a story Tom told just before the benediction. He said that sometime during her illness, Christine had said that when the end came, whenever that might be, she wanted her sister-in-law Shelley to be present. So, when it became apparent that Christine was in her last days, Shelley left her home in Durham and flew to Florida. She arrived one evening and went straight to a motel. Early the next morning, just after 6:30, Tom called Shelley on her cell phone. He knew she was an early riser and figured she'd be up. "Where are you?" he asked. "I'm here," she said. "I know you are here, but when are you going to be over here?" "I am here," she repeated. "Open the curtains. You will see." Tom pushed aside the curtains, and there she was, standing on the patio.

When I heard this story, I thought to myself, that's a perfect Tara story. Tara is the beloved female Buddha of Tibet and is the Buddha of compassionate action. Tara is depicted sitting on a moon cushion atop a lotus blossom. She sits cross-legged with her right foot extended, indicating that she is ready to come to our aid. In fact, it is said that when we call, she is already here.

Tom told the congregation at the memorial service that his wife was smart. She had known way ahead of time that in her dying she would have what she needed, but her husband and son would need Shelley. She was right. And when he called, she was already there.

Growing up as a Protestant, I was offered very few images of the feminine divine. No female entity was the object of my meditation or prayer. There was no powerful, holy, feminine being to whom I could appeal. Catholics had Mary, but Protestants were warned against devotion to anyone except God the father and his son Jesus. (I use male language here on purpose, with emphasis on father and son. No mothers are allowed.) For me, Mary was a pale background figure dressed in washed-out blue. As an adult, I've been left to reinvigorate stories of women in the Bible or borrow female figures from other religions.

I am so glad for the current series of RCWMS programs on the Feminine Divine, because I am learning more stories about sacred feminine figures like Tara and Kali. In October, Rachael Wooten led a meditation retreat that focused on Tara. In November, Mary Love May and Anita McLeod led a workshop on Kali. I've already told you a little about Tara, so now I'll tell you a bit about Kali.

I have known of Kali for many years, but I only had a vague sense of her as a wrathful Hindu goddess who, like Mother Earth, eventually consumes all living things. I was uncomfortable with the wrathful goddess. As a female and a Christian, I had been taught that rage and anger were bad. The story of Jesus overturning the tables of the moneychangers in the synagogue was the only one I knew that suggested a holy person could be angry.

Fortunately, other religions are not so reluctant to include the dark emotions or angry, wrathful deities in their understanding of the holy. When I get as angry as I was in early November, I would like for some furious, blazing goddess like Kali to come to my aid. Mary Love told a story about Kali in the workshop this fall that helps me imagine just such a thing. A version of the story appears in China Galland's *The Bond Between Women*. It goes something like this.

There was a time when the world was at the brink of destruction. Rivers dried up, all dancing stopped, demons roamed freely, and the gods could not stop them. So the gods retreated to the Himalayas where they remembered a teaching that said only a woman could save the world from this sort of destruction. So the gods shot forth streams of fire that converged in a pillar of flame as tall as the mountains themselves. Out of the fire came the Great Goddess Durga, riding a lion, wearing the crescent moon on her head. Durga quickly defeated thousands of demons and returned to her throne in the Himalayas. But the demons did not give up. Instead of trying to defeat her in battle, the Lord of the Demons and his younger brother tried to woo her. They asked her to marry them. She declined, saying she had vowed only to marry one who could defeat her in battle. Enraged, the Lord of the Demons commanded his forces to attack, but Durga defeated them with a glance. The Lord of the Demons sent more forces and commanded them to drag Durga to him by her hair. That was the last straw. Durga got so furious that her face turned dark as a storm and Kali sprang forth from her brow. Kali, a hideous, angry, frightening creature with many arms and a flashing sword, finished the job, defeating thousands of demons and leaving only the Lord of the Demons himself. Durga then reabsorbed Kali and all of her female warriors and challenged the Lord of the Demons himself. Time stopped as the goddess and the demon fought, pitching and rolling across the sky. The cosmos groaned with the enormity of their encounter. When Durga finally slew the Demon, he fell from the sky and the world was safe at last.

So on Halloween, when the president nominated the right wing's first choice for the US Supreme Court, it felt like something akin to Kali sprang from my brow. I was so angry, angry in a new way from the ways I have been angry at presidents off and on for the last thirty-five years. It feels like I have been telling presidents my whole adult life to stop with the war-making. I started college in the late 1960s in the midst of the student protests against the Viet Nam War. I came of age to the background chant of "No More War."

I now think of Kali as full of anger, but life-giving anger. Outrage at the injustices of the world. We could do with a little more outrage at the present moment. I like that she carries a sword known as the sword of discernment, one that cuts through illusions. Durga had been strong and patient in her battle to heal the world, but when pushed to the edge, she let loose a fierce version of herself.

At a recent gathering of women friends, several women reported that they were tired of being nice. Being nice will only get us so far. We don't have to split the world into good and bad, we don't have to demonize those who disagree with us, but I think that the energy we get from feeling outrage over war, torture, violence, or destruction can give us the ability to act, to speak, to reach out to those in need, to stand in the path of galloping greed and disregard for human life.

After Durga defeated the demons, it is said that the gods crowned her Queen of the Universe. They asked her to stay and rule the world, but Durga would have none of it. She promised the gods and the people that there was nothing more to fear and said, "Do not worry. If the world is ever in danger of being destroyed again, I will return."

It is comforting to imagine that a goddess like Durga, Kali, or Tara would come to my aid or to the aid of the world. And whether I believe in such a being or not, the idea of one helps me remember that I can come to my aid and that we can come to the aid of the world every day. I can also remember that the God of my own Christian heritage promised not to leave us alone, but to send a comforter to be with us. I might even try calling that Holy Spirit by the name of one of my new goddess friends, and see what that brings.

Volume 26, Number 4, December 2005

ART

Art and the Feminine Divine: An Exhibit will be on display in multiple Durham venues April 21–May 14, 2006. Come to the opening reception on April 21, 6–9 p.m., in conjunction with Culture Crawl in Durham.

Art and the Feminine Divine will bring together a hundred artists whose work celebrates the many forms and faces of God the Mother, Lover, Creatrix. Sponsored by the Resource Center for Women and Ministry in the South, the exhibit reveals the many ways we celebrate and demonstrate the feminine divine. The artwork is both abstract and representational and includes pieces in fabric, collage, painting, and sculpture. Musical events, storytelling, and a meditation session will be held during the exhibit. (See below for a listing of events.)

The exhibit was inspired by Mary Love May. Several years ago, Mary Love began making and giving away small clay bowls that resembled goddesses. This process grew into the idea of an art project involving many artists and also became a way of honoring the spirit of her mother, Mary Shaw May, now eighty-three, who lives with Alzheimer's disease. No longer able to speak a clear sentence, Mary Shaw once wrote poetry, essays and stories about Earth and spirit, women, and her own life. May's idea for the exhibit is an extension of giving away her goddess bowls, and this exhibit is a way of spreading goddess seeds all over Durham.

Artwork will be on display through May 14 at multiple locations in Durham:

117 Market Street;
Transom Gallery, 305 E. Chapel Hill Street
The Scrap Exchange Gallery, 548 Foster Street
Okun-Stern Loft, 208 Rigsbee Street
Francesca's, 706 9th Street.

EVENTS

Friday, April 21, 6:00–9:00 p.m.
Opening Reception in conjunction with Culture Crawl. Begin at any of
our downtown Durham venues.

Sunday, April 23, 8:00 p.m.
Songs of the Feminine Divine: A Concert by Jewelsong, Blayloc Café

Saturday, April 29, 8:00 p.m.
Lise Uyanik and the Mobile City Band & STELLA, Blayloc Café

Wednesday, May 3, 7:30 p.m.
Moons and Mirrors: Sacred Fabric Art, slide/lecture by Jude Spacks,
Okun-Stern Loft

Saturday, May 6, 2:00 p.m.
Storytelling from Five Faiths, Okun-Stern Loft

Friday, May 12, 2:00 p.m.
Tara Meditation, led by Rachael Wooten, Okun-Stern Loft

The Art & the Feminine Divine Committee includes: Miriam Biber,
Sallye Coyle, Kathleen Hannan, Bryant Holsenbeck, Mary Love May,
Anita McLeod, Courtney Reid-Eaton, Candice Ryals, Jeanette Stokes,
Candace Thomas, Sue Versényi, and Ann Woodward.

We would like to give special thanks to Hopkins Design Group, RGG
Architects, Self Help Ventures Fund, Tema Okun & Tom Stern, The
Scrap Exchange, The Transom, Francesca's, Emily Wexler, and Jennifer
McGovern.

Exhibiting Artists: Kelly Adams, Kit Adcock, Cynthia Aldrich, Charron
Andrews, Brianna Atkins, Barbara Barnes, Susan Baylies, Margo Wiley
Bennett, Thomas Bermudez, Betsy Blair, Jeannette Brossart, Nicole
Brown, Shannon Bueker, Danny Cameron, Stephanie Campbell, Linda
Carmel, Nancy Corson Carter, Shabari Case, Valerie Clack, Debbie
Cohen, Sallye Coyle, Julie Dean, Dori DeSantis, Susan Draughon,
Martha Dyer, Lori Easterlin, Bruce Edwards, Ann Ehringhaus, Pam

Epperson, Judith Ernst, Grace Evans, Dale Evarts, Laura Farrow, Vernessa Foelix, B. J. Fusaro, Sara Gabrielson, Mickey Gault, Janice Geller, Andrea Gomez, Galia Goodman, Tamsen Moriah Coyle Hall, Kathleen Hannan, Alyssa Hinton, Louise Hobbs, Bryant Holsenbeck, Suzanne Holt, Emily Huffman, Bonnie Hummel, Ava Johnson, Amy Kellum, Carrie Knowles, Patricia Kosdan, Michelle Lanier, Marcy Litle, Melissa Manley, Dianne Masi, Mary Love May, Nancy Tuttle May, Valerie McGaughey, Zakia Virginia McGuire, Anita McLeod, Patricia Merriman, Carol Mackay Mertz, Eleanor Mills, Sandy Milroy, Ellen O'Grady, Libby Outlaw, Brydie Palmore, Delphine Peller, Martha Jane Petersen, Sally Pillsbury, Sudie Rakusin, Luna Lee Ray, Courtney Reid-Eaton, Laurel Reinhardt, Daphne Reno, Margaret Sartor, Ebeth Scott-Sinclair, Sculpting the Goddess Within Workshop, Elizabeth Shupe, Julia Simmons, Susan Simone, Sue Sneddon, David Sovero, Jude Spacks, Sue Speier, Julie Hilton Steele, Marie Summers, Gilda Morina Syverson, Candace Thomas, Dana Thompson, Melody Troncale, Sue Versényi, Karin Vyner-Brooks, James Ward, Adele Wayman, Kay Webb, Susan Wells, Bobby Wells, Martha Whitfield, Sherri Wood, Ann May Woodward, and Melissa York.

Volume 27, Number 1, April 2006

TRUTH

"Yes means yes, no means no, whatever I wear, wherever I go," we chanted as we marched the mile from the East Campus to the West Campus of Duke University on a recent April evening. Over five hundred of us showed up for the annual Duke Take Back the Night march. "What does survival look like?" one woman called out. "This is what survival looks like!" we responded as we walked four and five abreast, I with Miriam, Rose, and Megan—three friends still in their twenties.

The march was larger than usual this year—a response to newspaper reports a few days earlier of an alleged rape at a party of Duke lacrosse players. An exotic dancer hired to entertain at the party charged that three men trapped her in a bathroom and assaulted her. The male students claimed they were innocent and submitted to DNA testing. The woman is black. The three students are white, as are forty-six of the forty-seven team members.

I attended a candlelight vigil at sunset on the day the story appeared in the newspaper. Two hundred students, faculty, and townspeople gathered in front of the house where the party took place. Vigil organizers said we were there to support the courage of victims who speak out. I thought to myself at the time that whatever had happened, the wild drunken parties for which the team was known were exactly the kind of out-of-control situations that could lead to violence.

For years, neighbors have complained to police and university officials about Duke students' off-campus parties. One night a few years ago, I was awakened at 3:00 a.m. by some hollering outside. From my bedroom window, I could see students in the yard of the rental house across the street. One young man was standing in the middle of the street screaming obscenities at the top of his lungs. Another was peeing in my front yard.

The Take Back the Night march ended in front of Duke Chapel where we sat on cold flagstones to listen to a Speak Out. Several women told of having been raped at age thirteen, several more of being sexually assaulted by friends or boyfriends on campus. Men spoke of feeling helpless in the face of a girlfriend recovering from rape. One woman said, "I did not even know it was sexual assault. My friends had to explain it to me."

The crowd was reminded that the Duke Sexual Assault Support Services defines sexual assault as "any sex act against your will, without your consent, or when you are unable to freely give consent." Rape is "any sex act involving penetration of any body opening by any object, that is against your will, without your consent, or when you are unable to freely give consent."

From the first reports, I assumed the woman was telling the truth. More than thirty years of work by rape crisis and domestic violence advocates has taught us all to believe the victim. Thirty years ago, authorities might have ignored the claims of a divorced exotic dancer with a minor police record. The police, hospitals, the media and the public believed the woman's allegations. She had bruises to support her story. The local District Attorney promised to prosecute to the full extent of the law.

The fact that a third of the lacrosse team had been arrested for alcohol or noise violations also helped us believe the victim, as did a horrific e-mail the night of the party by a student who proposed another party at which strippers would be killed and skinned. The report that the lacrosse players' DNA was not found on the victim and the claims that the victim arrived at the party with bruises make us wonder about truth.

We live in a culture in which male violence is prevalent. We live in a country whose president acts like he can do whatever he wants to just because he can. He invaded Iraq on flimsy evidence because he and his crowd wanted to rearrange the Middle East to make it friendlier to western oil interests. Following this example young, drunk male students at an elite university sometimes act like they can do as they please and if they get caught, their daddies will get them off.

When I told someone that I assumed the woman was telling the truth and also assumed that the accused were innocent until proven guilty, she asked me how one could hold that tension.

I said, "Support the woman. Believe her." Assume she is telling the truth. That's the first thing. The question for public opinion and for the university is how to deal with the students. They have not yet been charged with a crime. It is not clear who was present at the party and who was not. The university could have done more, as in putting them all on probation until the facts are sorted out. The students have lawyers who seem to have told them not to say anything about the case. The legal system and the values of community get crossways with each other pretty quickly in cases like this one.

The thing that makes me hesitate is that in my work against the death penalty, I have learned to reserve judgment about guilt. We've wrongly executed numbers of people in this country. I've stopped assuming that I know who is innocent and who is guilty.

It is hard to hold the tension in this case. The race, class, and gender inequities are huge. Still, even disgusting macho students have civil rights to be protected. They could be expelled on the basis of the out-of-control party alone, but the university has chosen for years not to take harsh actions about such parties. One question is whether the university contributes to violent, criminal behavior by not trying to stop these wild parties and drunken male behavior.

What seems right is that the public, most students, and the press assumed from the beginning that the woman was telling the truth. That would not have been the case thirty years ago.

People on campus, in town, and on listservs have been arguing with each another over who is right. I'm trying to find another approach.

Volume 27, Number 1, April 2006

BIRDSEED

One Saturday morning in mid-May, I was sitting in my backyard listening to the chatter of birds in the pecan tree overhead and the squeak of a swing in the park next to my house. I was tired and thrilled to be still. It was the last weekend of Art and the Feminine Divine and I had not spent enough time being quiet all year. The breeze was gorgeous. A storm earlier that week had cleared the air and lowered the temperature. It was a perfect May morning.

I sat on a black wrought-iron chair that I had bought, along with its twin and a side table, from a friend when she moved to a downtown loft a year or two ago. I took the chairs home and plopped them down under the only tree in my backyard, where they have remained. I've had a variety of pieces of furniture in the backyard in the last fifteen years: folding beach chairs, a hammock that was stolen, a lovely wooden garden bench that rotted, but nothing has been quite so satisfying as the wrought-iron chair in which I was sitting. I used to hang out on the front porch where there are two great rockers, but this spring, because of the chairs and lovely new paths in my garden, I rediscovered the fine southern art of sitting in the yard. I knew it would not continue for long, as the mosquitoes were on their way. But for that moment, all I wanted was to be in my own backyard. Who knew that two chairs and some garden paths could make such a difference?

I was watching the little birdhouse-shaped birdfeeder that hangs in the garden. I had put it out of commission the year before after losing a struggle with squirrels, but having acquired a large bag of seed from my neighbor Danny who moved to Mexico, I decided to get the feeder out and try it again. The squirrels had not yet attacked it, the birds seemed to enjoy it, and I was happily watching the birds as they flew back and forth, ate the seed or perched on the tall wrought-iron crook that holds up the feeder.

I concocted a theory that the squirrels had left the feeder alone this year because Danny's bag of seeds was all seed. My seed the year before had included cranberries and peanuts, which was like hanging a blinking neon sign on the feeder saying, "Step right up. Get your red hot squirrel food here."

The problem with squirrels is not so much that they eat the seed, but that they are so heavy they tip the feeder to one side and all the seed falls out. I had made attempts in the past to outsmart squirrels, and had learned what experts will confirm: squirrels are smarter than humans. So, when the squirrels took to the feeder last year, instead of trying to prevent them from raiding it, I just took it down.

Spring came again and along with it Danny's big new bag of seed that made me want to try again. I fished the small wooden house-shaped feeder out of a dark corner in the garage, lifted its hinged roof, poured in the seed, and hung it back on the wrought-iron crook, which I had never bothered to move from its place in the garden. Before long there were birds perched on the tiny porches, happily pecking at the seed that falls down through the house and spills out into reach. It's an ingenious design, but the birds are not very good housekeepers. They seem to crack the seeds and leave the hulls on the porch, like fans shelling peanuts at a baseball game. Subsequent birds have to throw the hulls off the porch to get to good seed. I assume it is as irritating to a bird as finding a sink full of dirty dishes would be to me.

I've been too busy this spring. I have not written much, except newsletter articles when I had to, and I've made no art at all. I've had so much work to do, but even so, I know that there is no one to blame for the shape of my life but myself. There are twenty-four hours in every day and I am the person responsible for how I use them. Yes there are the demands of work, relationships, eating, and sleeping, but I am in charge of my decisions. If I take on too many commitments, projects that are too big, friends who are too demanding, if I set a standard for my garden or my housecleaning that is too high, if I answer the phone every time it rings or answer all the e-mail when it arrives in my in-box, only I am to blame. I can't blame the weeds or the dust or the callers or even the large projects.

So I am going to begin again at the beginning. I am going to write in my journal for twenty or thirty minutes early every morning instead of checking my e-mail first thing. I am going to type three hundred words into the computer. I am going to make art, even bad art. I'm going to leave town for at least six weeks this summer. And I'm going to do a lot more of what I was doing that Saturday morning in mid-May: sit in my backyard watching the breeze dance through tall flowers while the birds throw empty hulls from their feeder.

Volume 27, Number 2, July 2006

GLEANING

A seventy-five-year-old pecan tree shades my backyard, house, and part of the park next door. Most years, after the weather turns cold, the pecans begin to fall. Last year produced such a good crop that I had nuts raining on the house and carpeting the ground. I had to watch my step as I walked from the house to the garage, even though I cleared the path almost every day.

On cold fall mornings, I often see elderly people looking for nuts in the park next door. I figure that the nuts that fall in my backyard belong to me and the ones that land in the park belong to anyone who wants to pick them up. Last year there were plenty for everyone. I shelled them, ate them, gave them away, and even put a few in the park to ensure that everyone would have some to pick up.

This summer, I spent several weeks in Santa Fe, New Mexico, looking after my friend Martha's house and dog. On one of my first walks around the neighborhood with Greta the dog, I noticed apricot trees that were dropping their fruit in the street. At first I stepped over the fallen fruit, but then gave myself permission to pick some up, hoping that the tree owners felt about their yield the way I do about my pecans.

Back in my borrowed kitchen, I admired the small ovals, red on one side and a rosy yellow on the other, and wondered if they were safe to eat. Their only flaw was that they were slightly squished on one side from falling on the pavement. I long ago stopped demanding perfect fruits and vegetables. Fruits and vegetables never used to look perfect, and I figured ten apricots smashed on one side were equal to five whole ones. Still, I found myself wondering whether there was such a thing as an ornamental poisonous apricot that would rot my stomach from the inside out.

I was startled to realize that I am totally dependent on grocery stores and farmers' markets to figure out what is edible. I am several generations removed from the land. Some of my grandparents and great grandparents would have known immediately what to make of the lovely found apricots.

In *The Omnivore's Dilemma*, Michael Pollan explores the history and politics of eating as he follows four American meals from field and forest to the table. In it he points out how ignorant we have become in this country. Many of us are poorly equipped to make sensible choices about what to eat. We have lost track of some of the wisdom of our various cultures—things like eating wasabi with raw fish to kill parasites or horseradish with pork for the same reason. If we don't pay attention we are liable to eat meal after meal that is mostly high fructose corn syrup.

I ate the apricots this summer and nothing bad happened. They were, in fact, delicious, especially after I cut off the squished side. I also bought some at the farmers' market in Santa Fe, but I liked the ones I picked up off the ground even better. They seemed special in some way, like an unexpected gift. It made me wonder what other gifts I am offered each day that I step right over or simply fail to notice.

Volume 27, Number 3, November 2006

SUE

I gave the following remarks on September 16, 2006 at a memorial service for Sue Versényi. Sue lived in Carrboro, wrote and taught, and attended two of our Writing Weeks at the beach in 2005. She died of breast cancer on August 30, 2006. She was forty-nine years old. Gifts from Sue's friends and family will help RCWMS to publish a volume of her poetry next year.

Sue Versényi never agreed to die. She did not want to die. She wanted to live to see her children grow up. She wanted to watch her garden bloom summer after summer. She wanted to write more poems, make more quilts, and teach more children to read and write. She didn't want to die, and so for days, and then weeks, she simply refused to do so.

Sue was strong, kind, warm, loving, creative, generous, and hospitable. She was a mother who poured her heart and energy into the care and guiding of her daughters. She and Adam created a home in which the life of the family was central. They shared meals and conversations around the table; they celebrated birthdays and a variety of religious and cultural traditions; they welcomed friends and strangers. Sue and Adam built a life that could be the envy of many and, by God, Sue did not want to leave it.

The last time I was with Sue while she was fully communicative was one night in early August at the hospital after she had broken her leg. She would probably be dead in two weeks. (Proved that one wrong, as per usual.) Another doctor suggested there was more that could be done. She was in a lot of pain, and it had been a particularly stressful day. But in came the girls with new purchases from Look Out and from Old Navy to show their mother, and the hospital room became a fashion show. We all laughed and talked and commented on the color and texture of the clothes meant for school a few weeks later. Sue was ready for lots more years of that.

Sue surprised us all. She kept breathing past her wedding anniversary, past the first day of school, twelve days past the day when the hospice nurses announced she would certainly die that day. She kept breathing past my trip to Indiana, past Margie's weeklong trip to Seattle, clear into the holy woman Mother Meera's visit to North Carolina. No one understood why her body kept on. We may never understand.

When I wrote to a friend who is a hospice chaplain to express my wonder at her living so long beyond all predictions and to describe the mix of anxiety and impatience that many of us felt, he asked, "On whose schedule is she doing her dying?" Sue and her Creator were right on time, he assured me, and they were up to something that would probably only baffle the rest of us.

Watching Sue breathe on one of those last afternoons, I felt like I was watching a newborn with respiratory problems. With such a child, I might wonder why the tiny person bothered to make the effort. That is certainly what I wondered with Sue. It looked like such a painful struggle. I wondered, as others had, why she didn't seem to want to give up.

Give up? What are you, nuts? Sue? Give up? She clung to life, not in a fearful way, but in her own strong-willed, tenacious, insistent, stubborn, opinionated way. If ever I met a woman I wanted to be on MY side, it was Sue. Watching her, I was awed by the strength of the life force, and awed by Sue.

For weeks, she remained among us, living, even in what most of us thought was a pretty meager imitation of life, but living nonetheless, because it was what she wanted most to do. We should all be so lucky as to have a mother or a love or a sister or a friend who would fight *so* hard to be with us. She loved us, one and all. And we loved her. She will live on, in our hearts, always.

So might it be.

Volume 27, Number 3, November 2006

EGGS

There are little bits of colored eggshell and confetti on the carpet at our office. I've not been able to bring myself to clean them up, because they remind me of something I seem to enjoy remembering. Let me explain.

I stopped by my artist friend Bryant's house, at the end of February, to pick up gifts for Margie Hattori and Anita McLeod, trustees who were rotating off the RCWMS Board. Margie and Anita have shouldered much of the weight of the Resource Center for six years and the Board wanted to thank them with a gift. Bryant's handmade books, made of recycled materials, seemed appropriate. Beautiful to look at and pleasing to hold in the hand, the books are great to write in, because they open all the way and lie flat.

While I was looking through Bryant's stack of finished books, she and I started talking about another artist, Mary Margaret Wade, who is also on the RCWMS Board. Mary Margaret has been undergoing chemotherapy treatments that make her nauseated and tired. "Here, I have something for her!" said Bryant as she reached for three colorfully dyed eggs that looked like Easter eggs but had tissue paper glued over the ends. "Cascarones!" she announced. I screwed up my face and said, "What?"

Bryant explained that she had just been to visit a friend in San Miguel de Allende in Mexico for a week that included Ash Wednesday. There must be some sort of celebration similar to Mardi Gras, because people were having parties and cracking these brightly colored eggs over each other's heads.

Bryant went in the kitchen and returned with a pasteboard cylinder covered in green paper with the word tea on the side and began to put three eggs inside. I was so enamored with the container that I hardly noticed when she reached in her paper shredder to grab a handful of strips to stuff the cylinder and protect the eggs. Bryant's whole house is like an art studio. Everywhere you look there are beautiful and unusual things to see. My imagination gets a jump-start when I walk in the door, and if I don't want to make art when I arrive, I will by the time I leave.

I left Bryant's with two handmade books, a canister of eggs, and a smile on my face. When Mary Margaret came by the office a couple of days later, I told her I had something for her from Bryant, asked if I could demonstrate, and cracked one of the eggs over her head. Bryant had said they were filled with confetti but I was surprised by the amount of stuff that fell out on Mary Margaret's head, her jacket, and fluttered to the floor. She laughed and took the other two eggs home, where I expected she would put them on a shelf with other precious objects. But no, she knew a good thing when she saw it. Within days, she had cracked the remaining two over the heads of a couple of young Hispanic men who came to do some work on her house, who grinned and knew exactly what the cascarones were.

In the midst of a world of brokenness, we need to remember when and how to celebrate. We weren't put on this earth us just to struggle and to suffer, but also to know joy.

Volume 28, Number 1, March 2007

THIRTY

The evening before I turned thirty, I jumped in the car with a friend and rode from Greensboro to Raleigh. It was a whim. I wanted to do something impulsive before I got old. Just before leaving my apartment, I called another friend in Raleigh to say I was coming and needed a bed. When I reminded her it was about to be my birthday, she consented to the impromptu visit.

The Resource Center for Women and Ministry in the South is turning thirty this year. While it does not feel like the organization is old, it's certainly not a kid anymore. It amazes me to realize that our interns weren't even alive when we began in 1977. I think of the life of the Resource Center in decades. For the first decade we supported and connected women in and entering ministry and worked on the campaign to pass the Equal Rights Amendment. In the second decade, we sponsored annual conferences on feminist theology and on social justice issues, such as economic justice and violence against women. We also housed a program for two years called RESPONSE: A Religious Response to Violence Against Women and Children. As we began our third decade in 1997, our direction shifted again as we constructed a canvas labyrinth and turned our attention to creativity and spirituality. In an attempt to provide opportunities for renewal, especially for women well over thirty, we sponsored a variety of retreats and workshops on meditation, writing, art, menopause, and being over fifty.

Since we like to celebrate, we will probably say that everything that happens this year is in honor of our 30th anniversary. Some of the year's activities include programs, retreats, a book, and a movie. See the Calendar for a list of events for the year. This spring you will want to pay particular attention to two events led by women whom we have invited to North Carolina.

AUTOBIOGRAPHY OF THE SOUL: A Writing Workshop led by Sharon Doubiago, April 20–21, 2007 (Friday, 7:00–9:00 p.m., and

Saturday, 9:30 a.m.–4:30 p.m.). This workshop will put the creative back in creative writing and explore writing as a spiritual undertaking. Aimed at anyone writing poetry, memoir, personal essay, or fiction, the workshop will offer participants an opportunity to practice writing from the psyche, from the content of the self. Using memory, poetry, and exercises, we will identify our own stories, rhythms, dreams, issues, and voices. You will love award-winning writer Sharon Doubiago, who has written more than two dozen books and has been leading Autobiography of the Soul workshops for twenty years. Injured by her own experience in writing classes, she is gentle and inspiring to her students. Since she lives in San Francisco, we are thrilled to have snagged her on a rare trip North Carolina. You can read more about her at www.writersontheedge.org/doubiago.html.

LIKE A BURNING FIRE SHUT UP IN MY BONES: Women and the Prophetic Voice, April 28, 2007, 2:00–4:00 p.m., will be led by Carolyn J. Sharp, Associate Professor of Hebrew Scriptures, Yale Divinity School. Participants will examine the prophetic voices of several Hebrew prophets to assist in claiming our sources of authority, understanding our communities, and discerning when and how to speak a prophetic word to struggling communities and a suffering world.

We will publish a book of poetry by Sue Versényi. Sue wrote many of the poems in her collection, *Enough Room*, in 2005 when she attended two of our week-long writing retreats. She died in 2006. A student at the UNC Wilmington publishing lab is currently designing the book, which we plan to publish in September.

Our documentary project, *Meinrad Craighead: Praying with Images*, is proceeding apace. We anticipate its completion by the end of the year. In the last two years, we have raised $50,000 of our $100,000 budget for the documentary. Filmmakers Georgann Eubanks and Donna Campbell have recorded over thirty hours of interviews. Executive Producer Amy Kellum and intern Amanda Earp are planning twenty fundraising house parties for the spring and summer. We have created sets of greeting cards with two of our favorite Meinrad images to sell

(10 cards for $15). We also have Meinrad's retrospective book for sale, *Crow Mother and the Dog God*.

WISE CHOICES, a retreat for women over 50, will take place March 29–April 1. Anita McLeod and Margie Hattori have been leading workshops and retreats for women over 60 for the last few years with the post-menopausal crowd in mind. Women over 50 started saying that they wanted to be included, so beginning with the retreat in March, women over 50 will be included as well. The next retreat will be October 4–7.

We have two more week-long writing retreats scheduled this year in the Pelican House at Trinity Center on the North Carolina coast: April 29–May 6 and September 23–30. Just give a woman a week, a bed, food, silence in the daytime, and a few companions to talk with in the evenings and watch her go. After a day or two of rest, participants write long, funny, moving, or heartbreaking pieces that lead to interesting conversations, more resting, and more writing. We did not know what a good idea it was to have these retreats when we started them four years ago. A few of us were just desperate for enough quiet to get some work done. We had no idea it would also restore deeply worn and wounded places in our souls.

We promise an event on the Black Madonna this year. Board member Rachael Wooten has been leading programs on the Black Madonna for over a decade, most recently in Charlotte and Chapel Hill for Jungian groups. These were received with such enthusiasm that we've made her promise she'll do one for us. To learn about the Black Madonnas of Europe, read China Galland's *Longing for Darkness: Tara and the Black Madonna*.

Our new Board Chair, Debra Brazell, is from Louisiana and knows how to have a good time. Since her first response to the anniversary was, "Let's have a party," I expect we will. Stay tuned. It's only March and we don't actually turn thirty until August.

Volume 28, Number 1, March 2007

MARY MARGARET

The Saturday before Easter, I sat on Ruth's screened-in porch visiting
with her mother, Margaret Wade. Meanwhile, Margaret's other
daughter, my friend Mary Margaret, lay in a hospital bed at Duke
University Medical Center, having called the doctor and arranged
to be admitted when the tumor in her lung caused such shortness
of breath that she needed help breathing. I've liked Mary Margaret's
mother ever since she and Mary Margaret's grandmother came to visit
the Greensboro office Mary Margaret and I shared in the early 1980s.
I remember being struck by the two older women with smiling faces.
They seemed sturdy and kind. And their story was so interesting.

The grandmother had grown up in Alaska as the daughter of a
missionary. And not just any missionary. John Killbuck was a Native
American from Ohio and a Moravian missionary. When Mary Margaret
and her mother went to Alaska in 1999, the people in the remote village
where the missionary had preached knew all about him. The Killbuck
mountain range is even named for him.

I went to see Mrs. Wade that Saturday afternoon because I like her, but
also because she was facing a mother's worst nightmare. Her daughter
had terminal cancer and the end was palpably near. I had nothing to
offer Mrs. Wade except myself, and an ear if she wanted to talk. We are
fond of one another. She likes that I helped look after Mary Margaret
when she had surgery for uterine cancer four and a half years ago and
she brings me tokens from time to time: wild rice at Christmas, bubbles
in an egg-shaped bottle at Easter, a small white cotton quilt that I put
on my bed at the beach when I go there to write.

It was all breaking my heart. It broke my heart that I was losing my
friend, and it broke my heart that Margaret was losing her daughter.
Every mother should at least be able to hope that at her own death she
will look up into the loving faces of her children. Margaret lost her
husband Charles a dozen years ago and her only son a few years later,

leaving two daughters, Ruth and Mary Margaret, and one of them was slipping away.

We talked about Easter and whether Margaret, who gets around with the aid of a walker, would go to the sunrise service in the Sarah P. Duke gardens. I finally realized she was pulling my leg. We spoke of the beach. Mary Margaret's father, Charles, had grown up in Morehead City, just across the sound from where I go to write. Margaret still has a condo there, near the shipyard. Mary Margaret spent many summer weeks in the last ten years helping to build an environmental camp nearby at Cape Lookout. The camp closed at the end of last year and the director moved away.

Mary Margaret had been going to that part of the North Carolina coast all her life. I expect that was the first beach sand to touch her tiny feet. Born in late December 1948, she was probably just learning to sit up when the grownups placed her on a blanket facing the Atlantic Ocean or baptized her toes in the restless water. I doubt she ever thought about whether or not she loved the ocean. She just did. For the decade that she supported the camp at Cape Lookout, she was caring for the part of the earth that had fallen into the care of her ancestors, lighthouse keepers and fishermen who had navigated those waters. She did what she could to help educate younger generations about the delicate balance of life on the slender thread of islands that form the outer edge of our state.

While sitting on the screened porch asking questions so Mrs. Wade would tell stories, it occurred to me to ask when Charles had attended Duke. I knew he was a Duke graduate and had eventually served as a trustee. I had even attended a memorial service in Duke Chapel when he died. But I did not know how old he was or exactly when he was there. Mrs. Wade said he was born in 1915 and was in the class of 1938. I was wondering whether he might have been at Duke with my dad.

Though I have known Mary Margaret for almost thirty years, it had never occurred to me to ask about this before. We shared an office, served on the NARAL-NC board together, worked on RCWMS, taken trips to the beach, made art together, talked for hours about religion, politics, and lost marriages, but we rarely talked about our dads. When I first knew her in Greensboro, I was mad at my father for divorcing my mother when I was twelve and then dying when I was twenty-five. I didn't give a shit about the exact date he was in college or anything else he did. I wouldn't get interested in that sort of detail about him until my own divorce sent me searching for the father I had pitched out in a blind rage.

By the Easter Saturday I sat with Mrs. Wade, I had let my sweet father back into my heart, forgiven him for breaking it so often, and had become intensely curious about who he really was. I wondered if he and Charles Wade might have been in school together. Daddy only spent two years at Duke before his mother got mad at him over some indiscretion and made him come back to Georgia to finish at Mercer.

Class of 1938. Hmmm. I started counting backwards on my fingers. Mother and Daddy were married in 1944 in Dallas after he finished his medical residency. Was it two years of internship and residency and four years of medical school? Forty-four minus six is…what? It was too complicated. I can never do the math. The man was born ninety years ago in 1917 and who can add or subtract when there's a seven involved. I gave it up and promised myself to look up my father's class year at some point. Margaret's daughter was dying. I could figure out graduation years some other time.

In early May, I went to the beach for a week of quiet and writing. One morning while walking on the beach, I was thinking of Mary Margaret. Her feet would more than likely never touch the sand again. She was back home from the hospital by then but could hardly get from the bed to the bathroom without help. Maybe heaven would be like the beach, I mused—warm sand, gentle waves, bright sun, and a slight breeze. Yes, surely if heaven existed it would be just like that. And that distant blue line, where the sea meets the sky, that must be where Mary Margaret was going. Out there where we couldn't quite see, out there where it looked straight and flat and sure.

Back inside after my walk, I remembered the question about college dates and looked in my computer. Sure enough, my father was in the class of 1938. He arrived at Duke University in the fall of 1934 from Savannah, Georgia, another city by the sea, the same time Charles Wade traveled inland from Morehead City. What are the chances they knew one another? Better than even, but we will never know. My father left after his sophomore year, returned to Georgia, and eventually headed west. Charles Wade spent his working life in Winston-Salem, where he raised a family with Margaret and worked for R. J. Reynolds Tobacco Company. Whether the two men ever met or not, they walked the same ground for a couple of years. What we do know is that years later their daughters became friends, and that we, like our fathers, love the sea.

Sometime in her last weeks, I told Mary Margaret that I like to think that after we die we go back to where we were before we were born and that the damp unknown from which I emerged has never seemed like a bad place. She said she was not afraid of that, just about the "ramp up" to it.

As I turned from my computer to look out a window to the sea, a dolphin broke the surface not far off shore and I thought to myself, "There's the very creature that can take Mary Margaret away. When the end comes, may God's sleek messenger carry my friend out beyond the horizon."

Mary Margaret Wade slipped away in the early hours of a Sunday morning in June.

Volume 28, Number 2, June 2007

CELEBRATIONS

Thirtieth Anniversary Luncheon

The Resource Center for Women and Ministry in the South turned thirty years old in August this year. The Sallie Bingham Center for Women's History and Culture at Duke hosted a luncheon in our honor on Thursday, September 6, 2007. Friends and colleagues gathered in the Rare Book Room at Perkins Library to share memories of RCWMS and enjoy tasty treats. The Resource Center's papers have been archived at the Bingham Center for fifteen years.

Laura Micham, Director of the Bingham Center, welcomed everyone. Jeanette Stokes gave a brief history of RCWMS; Anita McLeod read from *Enough Room*, Sue Versényi's collection of poems that RCWMS just published; Debra Brazzel offered reflections on the Meinrad Craighead Documentary Project; and Rachael Wooten commented on the interfaith work of RCWMS.

In addition to the RCWMS papers, the Bingham Center has archived papers of former RCWMS board members Nancy Peeler Keppel, Mary Margaret Wade, and Bett Hargrave.

Enough Room by Sue Versényi

RCWMS is pleased to announce the publication of *Enough Room*, poetry by Sue Versényi. On Sunday afternoon, September 9, forty-five people came to Market Street Books in Chapel Hill, North Carolina, for a reception for the book.

Sue Versényi was born in New Haven, Connecticut, and moved to Carrboro, North Carolina, in 1988. She earned her BA from Hampshire College and an MFA in Creative Writing from Warren Wilson College. Sue had a thriving private practice in Carrboro as a reading and writing specialist and coach. An artist in many mediums, she was a published poet, an exhibited fabric artist, and an avid gardener. Sue died of breast cancer in 2006, leaving behind her husband Adam, two teenaged daughters, Elena and Nina, and scores of friends. She was forty-nine.

In this bittersweet collection of poems, Sue reflects on the body, nature, family, love, and living with cancer. Many of the poems were written in 2005 at the beach during RCWMS-sponsored writing weeks. Spare and deep, these poems will take up residence in your heart.

To order *Enough Room* by Sue Versényi (RCWMS, 2007), send $19 (includes tax & shipping) to: RCWMS, 1202 Watts Street, Durham, NC 27701, or see www.rcwms.org.

Meinrad Craighead Documentary Project

On the last day of August, twenty people gathered at Anita McLeod's house to see a ten-minute preview of the Meinrad Craighead documentary and to enjoy food and conversation. We've had fourteen house parties for the documentary project this year, which have raised $12,000. We have now reached $80,000, on our way to the goal of $100,000. People have been wonderfully generous. This fall filmmakers Georgann Eubanks and Donna Campbell will be editing the final version of the film, which will be released in 2008.

For more information about the Meinrad Craighead Documentary Project, see www.MeinradProject.org.

Volume 28, Number 3, September 2007

CREEK

Rachael called and asked if I wanted to go to Asheville with her for a weekend in August. She was half joking, and I said, "No." I had just returned from ten days in Oklahoma and Texas, and I did not want to go off anyplace else. It's a four-hour drive to Asheville. Rachael owns thirty-eight acres north of Asheville, near Hot Springs, North Carolina, and she likes to go up that way a couple of times a year.

Then I thought about it. The weekend she suggested was the same weekend Dwight was planning to drive his daughter to her college near Asheville. I could ride up with Rachael on Friday, spend the night with my friends Lucy and Tom in their new house in south Asheville, Dwight could come on Saturday, and then he and I could drive back to Durham on Sunday. It started sounding like fun. So I said, "Yes, probably." This being a last-minute sort of plan, I kept saying we would just lean in that direction.

Rachael called her favorite B&B in Hot Springs to reserve a room. Lucy said she'd be happy to see us and to have any combination of us stay with her. In recent years, I've learned to have more ease, to struggle less, and to walk through doors that open. The doors to this little adventure seemed to swing wide open, and sure enough on a Friday in August, Rachael and I got in her red Subaru station wagon and headed for the mountains.

I complained for the first half of the trip, because I did not like the seats in Rachael's car, but after stuffing several pillows under my butt, I shut up about it.

We arranged to meet Lucy in downtown Asheville and arrived in time to spend a few minutes in Malaprops, that city's wonderful independent bookstore. After a delicious dinner, Rachael headed to Hot Springs and Lucy and I went to her house where Tom was returning from a meeting and we all settled in for a night's rest.

On Saturday morning, Lucy and I went back into downtown Asheville where I bought a pair of winter shoes and some yarn for my newest cool weather hobby: knitting. Then we started up the windy road to Hot Springs to join Rachael for lunch and to see her land.

From the moment we arrived at Rachael's favorite B&B I was charmed by the place. The Duckett House Inn is a stately two-story clapboard house with a big front porch that sits on a rise above Spring Creek. The two men who own the place have loved on it for seventeen years, and it shows. The yard, the house, the furnishings, the hand-built barn, the simple well-equipped kitchen, all radiate love and a commitment to place and to quality. Hot Springs is a tiny community, near the Appalachian Trail, surrounded by miles and miles of forest. It was the site of a popular nineteenth century spa, which burned, but you can still take the baths and drink the mineral water at the location of the old spa in the center of town. I loved everything about Hot Springs, which I will now think of as the Ocracoke of the mountains.

We pulled chairs around a small table on the front porch of the inn, got out our picnic foods, and had lunch in a most delightful setting. A generous yard with a plot of sorghum to one side stretched out in front of the inn. Hummingbird feeders hung in low branches nearby. I was as happy as I could be to sit quietly, eat my lunch, stare out at the lawn and trees, and watch the hummingbirds come and go.

That might have been outing enough for me. I could have stayed on that porch all afternoon, writing and resting. I did not have my laptop computer, but Rachael had hers and the inn had wireless Internet access. I could have been happy right there for many hours, but Rachael was determined we should see her land.

Off we went on another winding mountain road. After half an hour of zigging and zagging and my repeated questions about how much longer I was going to have to slosh around in the backseat of the car, we arrived at Beasley's Cove, the rural neighborhood that includes Rachael's property.

The land is in a beautiful spot with wooded mountain ridges, a pleasant view, and a cleared area that once held a home place. Though I'm sure

Rachael would have liked to have stayed longer, the gnats were biting. After Lucy stirred up a hornet's nest and got stung a few times, we surveyed the clearing and left.

Though I think of myself as loving the out-of-doors, my favorite part of the day so far had been the civilized inn. I still had great expectations for the swim in Spring Creek, which I had been promised. I hoped that would make up for the zigzag roads and the pesky gnats.

Rachael took us to a lovely spot on the creek where she likes to swim, but the "swimming hole" looked more like a wading area to me. "Is this where you swim?" I asked. To which Rachael offered the obvious explanation: the summer drought had drained the normally chest-deep water so that it was only knee high.

I waded into the creek and squatted down in about six inches of water, slipped on the wet rocks under my feet, and splash, I was in up to my neck. I was horizontal, not vertical, mind you, but at least I was wet. A narrow place between a couple of boulders nearby made a nice shoot and some other swimmers showed us how they had been shooting the rapids on their backs. That was so much fun I stopped being cranky about not really being able to swim. It was a beautiful spot and there were plenty of places to sit in the water, lie back, get wet, and admire the sky. I had wanted to put my foot in a cold mountain stream and that longing had been satisfied.

After a fabulous dinner at yet another inn in Hot Springs, Lucy and I filled jugs with mineral water at the site of the old spa and returned to Asheville. I counted the day as a huge success. I've been told that if you play, you will get hurt. If you allow yourself to encounter the natural world, you will probably get bit, stung, or banged up. You might also find that afterwards your heart has opened a little wider, that you have been in the presence of the holy, and you have fallen in love with the world all over again. I did.

Volume 28, Number 3, November 2007

KEEP GOING

It's true what I learned when I was in college.

I was about twenty when I attended my first Zen Buddhist sesshin (meditation retreat). I remember only a few things about the weekend retreat held in the Field House at Smith College. One is the crack in the floor, which I observed for hours on end. Another is that when it was over I said to myself, "I've done that now. Won't have to do that again." The most striking thing I remember, however, is an instruction given by the Japanese roshi (teacher) who led the weekend. He said that when we listened to his teachings, we did not need to struggle to remember what he said. He promised that anything of real use to us would find its way inside of us and take root. He was right. The one thing I remember he said is that I didn't have to struggle to remember what he said.

In October this year, we had a small flood at my house. Our washing machine hose burst, which would have been messy enough had the washing machine been in the basement or on the first floor, but it is on the second floor. No one was home at the time, so the black rubber serpent spewed water for several hours. When Dwight came home just after 5:00 that Friday afternoon, he was greeted by a waterfall cascading from the second floor landing down into the hallway below and water raining through the ceiling of the study just off the hall.

Before I got home that day from a quick trip to Winston-Salem, Dwight had turned off the water, dragged the study's soggy throw rug out onto the front porch and draped it over the banister, and sopped up all the visible water with towels and buckets.

As I write, the study has been cleared of furnishings, the ceilings have been torn out in the hallway and the study, and the wall between the hall and the study has been removed. I can enter the study through the doorway or simply slip between the studs. And yes, the insurance company will help pay for the unplanned renovations.

As you can imagine, there was a lot of wet paper in a room we called "the study." One soggy pile contained rejection letters from agents I tried before I found one who agreed to represent *Hurricane Season*, a book I have finished about recovering from divorce. (Fortunately, my computer was in the car. Dwight was not so lucky. His laptop was in the study and when he picked it up, water poured out of it. It's a goner.)

Since we had to move everything out of the study, boxes and piles of paper wound up in the dining room. In the evenings after the flood, I sorted piles. I allowed myself one basket of things I simply couldn't throw away, but the rest of it I recycled or filed. While sorting, I came across a stack of quarterly newsletters from the North Carolina Writers Network, which I had saved because one of them contained a Judy Goldman quote I wanted to keep. But which one? I spread three years of the newsprint circulars out in front of me on the floor and leafed through them. As I went, I found other useful articles to clip, a danger of taking too close a look at an old pile. Nonetheless, I found the interview with Judy Goldman in a 2004 issue.

Here's the quote.

> Perseverance is what it's all about. It's not really about talent. There are a lot of people with a lot of talent, but not a lot of people with perseverance. It's all about staying with it, no matter which part of the process you're engaged in, whether it's the writing of the book—so many people begin a novel and don't finish it…. Then when you get to the publishing process, it's so easy to give up…. It's all about perseverance and staying with it.

As a child I discovered that if I stuck with a club or a camp long enough, eventually they would let me be in charge. As a young adult, I learned that the people who get PhDs are the ones who don't give up. Later on, writers assured me that writing is really slow work and not to become discouraged. Judy Goldman assured me of that. Don't give up. Keep going.

It took from 1995 to 2002 to finish and publish *25 Years in the Garden*, a book of my essays from South of the Garden, and that was after most of the essays had already been written. With *Hurricane Season*, it took five years to get over the separation and divorce enough to even look at my journals, and then four years to write the book, cut a hundred pages, get other people to read it, and rewrite it several times.

When writing, I frequently hear a voice in my head saying, "This is junk. Why are you still working on this?" I reply, "Maybe so, but this is what I am doing and I am going to keep going." I try to finish a project and then let people I respect help me decide if it is worth publishing. I'm telling you this in case you write and think your writing is garbage. Read it out loud. Get into a writing group. Share it with someone else. How will anyone ever know what your life is like if you don't tell them? If you need help with the prose, there are people around who are more than willing to assist you.

And as for whether you are writing the right thing or not, it's not really up to you or to me. Just keep going. And pray. You might use Thomas Merton's prayer, "My Lord God, I have no idea where I am going…and the fact that I think I am following Your will does not mean that I am actually doing so. But I believe that the desire to please You does in fact please You."

Finally, it is not the goal, but the journey that is important. It is not the finished piece, but the writing of the piece that changes me. Writing a book, looking for a lost quote, and repairing a house are all part of the journey. If we seek our own deep wisdom, trust a community of friends, and rely on the presence of the Holy One, then we may discover again and again that the journey is home.

It's like the roshi was saying: don't struggle. Just listen and you will hear and remember whatever is really important. Life does not have to be such a struggle. Just keep going. There is no road ahead. We make the road as we go.

Volume 28, Number 4, December 2007

H⊙PE

I'm taking a Duke class, The South in Black and White, taught by Tim Tyson, a white guy from North Carolina with a PhD in African American history, who is best known for his book *Blood Done Sign My Name*. I thought I knew something about the history of the South. After all, I am descended from southerners in every direction. Reading about slavery, white supremacy, lynchings, burnings, and every manner of human evil after Reconstruction and in the Jim Crow South, made me feel like people are simply horrible creatures.

In the class I learned that there was a coalition called the Fusion Coalition in North Carolina in the early 1890s that had been successful in electing black and white officials to state and local offices. The short version of the story is that Josephus Daniels, who would later own the *Raleigh News & Observer*, the paper of record in North Carolina, and Charles B. Aycock, who would later be the governor of North Carolina, and their white supremacist buddies marched into Wilmington, burned the black newspaper building, shot some African Americans, and herded others to the train station, telling them never to come back. In an armed coup, they ousted Coalition leaders all over the state, forcing elected officials to resign or flee on the spot.

One of the assignments for the class was to do research on my hometown. "Tulsa, Oklahoma, how boring," I thought. "Nothing ever happens there." In looking online, I was reminded of a race riot in Tulsa in 1921. I had not known of the riot until a commission was appointed a decade ago to study what had happened. After interviewing survivors (children at the time of the riot) and doing extensive historical and archeological work, the commission determined that the Tulsa Riot (better thought of as a massacre) was the deadliest race riot in the history of the country, and the only time aerial bombing had taken place on US mainland soil.

The riot was set off by an incident in which a black man probably bumped into a white female elevator operator. She screamed and he ran from the building. He was then arrested and accused of rape. Determined not to let the man be lynched, the police chief and his deputies barricaded themselves in the courthouse as a large mob of white men gathered outside. A smaller crowd of black men gathered in Greenwood, the African American part of Tulsa, and went down to the courthouse to protect the accused. Some gun was fired and a riot broke out. Thousands of white males armed with shotguns, rifles, and pistols stormed into Greenwood.

Estimates are that 150 to 300 people died, though death certificates exist for only thirty-nine. Some think it could have been as many as 3,000. Thirty-five blocks of Greenwood were burned to the ground. Black people were shot in the street, dragged from their homes, and rounded up like criminals. Others simply walked out of town and never came back.

Reading about the racial history of Tulsa was anything but boring. I was horrified. In the face of all that, I wondered whether there were any signs of hope.

Recently, I had lunch with a friend who is an avid watcher of presidential campaigns. We celebrated the fact that two Democratic candidates are a white female and a black man. She commented that there is hope springing up around the Barack Obama campaign. She noted that some people still have John Kennedy's picture hanging in their homes, not because he was such a great president (she didn't think he was) but because they remember how they felt when he was president. Hopeful, they felt hopeful.

A few days later I ran across a *Time* magazine article about the interest of young people in presidential campaigns. *Time* reported that in 2000 thirteen percent of eighteen- to twenty-nine-year-olds polled were paying attention to the presidential campaign. In 2004 it was twenty-four percent, and this year it is seventy-four percent. Nearly half of the young people polled said they were "passionate and deeply committed to a particular presidential candidate."

Later, at a continuing education event at Duke I met Tom and Farra Cottingham. Both Duke grads, they are eighty-nine and ninety-one years old. I learned that Tom was from Georgia and Farra from Oklahoma, as am I. As we talked around a lunch table, it became clear that they were both very progressive. When I asked him how he could be so progressive and have grown up in Georgia, he said it was because of his father. His dad held up a grand jury for three days one time while resisting the pressure to convict a black man. "They threatened him," Tom said. "We're going to get you." They never did.

These are signs of hope. A man born in the 1880s standing up against white supremacy. A coalition of black and white people in North Carolina in the 1890s working together to get people elected. A white woman and a black man in a contest to be their party's candidate for president in 2008.

Change is slow, and as Sr. Evelyn Mattern once said to me, the price of justice is constant vigilance.

Volume 29, Number 1, March 2008

CARTER

Seventeen years ago, the phone rang and a friend's voice said, "Carter has had a heart attack. We are not sure if she will survive. Please come." I was standing in the condominium on Gregson Street that my first husband and I had rented for several months that winter while we looked for a house to buy in Durham. The heavy Spanish-revival furniture we had in that dining room is forever burned into my memory along with my saying, "I have to go to Winston-Salem. I'll be back sometime."

Anne Carter Shelley was one of my first Presbyterian clergywomen friends. She followed her first husband to Durham where he had a job, shortly after I finished seminary at Duke and moved to Greensboro. Though we never lived in the same city at the same time, we became close friends.

Carter went about finding a call for herself in the most systematic, energetic way I have ever seen. She wrote nearly every parish minister in the Presbytery, introduced herself, said she was looking for a job and explained what she could do for them right then.

When a call came from the Butner Presbyterian Church, she gave it her whole heart. She tried to organize all sorts of programs and was disappointed to discover that the federal employees who made up the membership of the church only wanted church services on Sunday morning and not much more. When her first husband came home one day, said he had met someone on an airplane, fallen in love, and was leaving her, she was cared for and supported in the most wonderful way by her otherwise not very enthusiastic congregation.

Single again, Carter rented an apartment designed for a handicapped person. While she was not disabled, she enjoyed the bathroom that was so large she could do her exercises in it. Always more interested in ideas than housework, she forgot to buy a vacuum cleaner for the apartment.

The carpets were new, and I teased her for years about the fuzz balls that rolled around the floors.

Eventually she became the associate minister at First Presbyterian Church in Durham. We were central to one another's lives for the better part of three decades. We served as co-chairs of the Committee on Women's Concerns in our presbytery. She participated in my ordination in 1982. When I married my first husband in 1990, she served as one of the clergy. When she got married a second time, I was one of the ministers in her wedding.

Carter left First Presbyterian in Durham to pursue a PhD in preaching at Princeton Theological seminary but was not thrilled with the program, and her health was declining from kidney disease. When she returned to North Carolina, she did some work with me at the Resource Center for Women and Ministry in the South until she figured out what to do next. Eventually she chose a PhD program in rhetoric in the English Department at UNC Greensboro, which was an alternative way to study preaching. She went on to serve more churches and to be an Associate Executive Presbyter.

We often joked about the three Presbyterian clergywomen who had served in North Carolina: Carter Shelley, Shelley Wiley, and Wiley Smith. My friends were always getting them mixed up. "Now which one is she?" they would ask when I was talking about one of the three. Both Carter and Shelley had served on the board of RCWMS and Wiley had been to several of our retreats.

I didn't see Carter as often after 1995, when she married Tom Frazer, a crunchy granola doctor in Wilkesboro, North Carolina, and moved there to help raise his two children. I visited her new home several times and saw her whenever she came to the Triangle. She taught English part time in Boone and Winston-Salem and pastored more congregations. Last year, with the children launched and out of the house, Tom and Carter decided they wanted an adventure and moved to Orcas Island in the Puget Sound where he joined a practice. She was writing a memoir about being a stepparent and was pursuing work in the church. He said she was the perfect partner for him.

After receiving that phone call seventeen years ago, I went speeding to the hospital in Winston-Salem. Carter was stable by the time I arrived. The doctors convinced her it was a one-time event brought on by the stress of the surgery and not to worry about her heart. Eighteen months ago she had another cardiac episode but was told that reducing life stress and keeping up her exercise program (she was once a dancer and had become an avid walker) was the best medicine.

On Saturday morning, February 9, 2008, she was back in the Carolinas visiting her family and went to an exercise class in Rock Hill, South Carolina, where she had grown up. She collapsed during the class, could not be revived, and was gone forever. The world lost a vibrant, generous, kind, engaged woman, a wife, stepmother, minister, daughter, sister, and friend. She is survived by her parents, four siblings, her husband, two stepchildren, and scores of friends.

Carter's memorial service was held at Oakland Avenue Presbyterian Church in Rock Hill, South Carolina, on Wednesday, February 13. Carter was still a member of Salem Presbytery when she died. Dozens of clergy attended the service. I helped to lead the service along with clergywomen Laura Smith Conrad, Dale Walker, and Jamie Pharr, and graduate school friend Warren Rochelle.

When we left Rock Hill after the service, it was just beginning to drizzle. Not far up the highway, it started to rain, though the sun was shining. We were right on the edge of the storm. "Look!" said Lori Pistor who was riding with me, "A rainbow." Just to our right was the beginning of a gorgeous rainbow and before long the other end appeared to our left. As we rolled along in the rain, the end of the rainbow moved until it was literally laid out on the pavement in front of us. Carter would have liked the rainbow road. Later, we stopped for something to eat in Greensboro, and when we came out of the restaurant it was snowing hard. Big fluffy snowflakes settled on our coats like a benediction for the day.

Volume 29, Number 1, March 2008

PILGRIM

What I learned from a week in Spain and ten days in France this spring
is that I like being a pilgrim but I don't much like being a tourist. At
least that is what I kept saying to myself as I traipsed through ancient
cities and whizzed past mountains, vineyards, and sea.

While a tourist travels to visit sites, a pilgrim goes in search of the
divine. The wise pilgrim knows that the learning or meaning is as much
in the journey itself as in the destination. I know that when I am too
focused on the destination, I can miss a lot along the way, whether I am
on my way to the top of a mountain, the edge of the sea, or a morning
walk in Durham.

The parts of the trip to Spain and France that I enjoyed the most were
when I stopped to pay attention or got off the main path and wandered
around. For instance, the pilgrimage to the Abbey of Montserrat near
Barcelona was fascinating. I loved the 800-year-old wooden statue of
Mary and her young son that is the focal point of the church. I stood
before her with other members of our small group as we wept tears of
joy or loss or longing. I would not have traded seeing her for anything,
but what I will carry with me forever is the sound of the pealing bells
calling us and other pilgrims to prayer.

One morning on my way to Lauds, I stopped near the door to the
church, put my back to the outside wall, and let the sound of the bells
wash over me. Bong, bong, bong, bong—the enormous brass bells
clanged again and again—the sound bouncing off the stone walls of the
courtyard around me and reverberating from the great stone mountains
overhead. It was like being rolled in waves of sound.

A few days later, my husband and I were driving in the Camargue, the
agricultural area in the south of France below Arles. We left the main
road and followed the map to smaller and smaller roads, hoping for
an adventure. Near midday, we came to a ferry that crossed the Petit

Rhone (a branch of the Rhone), but could not cross because the ferry stops every day for lunch. Beside the dock, there was a small restaurant, the sort of place that in the US would serve greasy hamburgers and give you indigestion. In the south of France the tiny cafe served us delicious crepes, salad, and a fine glass of wine. We relaxed in the shade of an umbrella until it was time to take the five-car ferry across the narrow river. Later that afternoon, on another back road, we stopped at a fruit and vegetable stand, where we finally met a woman who spoke no English at all. It seemed like we had to drive to the very end of France to get away from traffic, tourists, and people who spoke English. We succeeded, not by going directly to a ferry or a produce stand, but by wandering around, slowly.

After a week in Provence, we took the fast train from Avignon to Paris. Arriving too late in the afternoon to take in a museum, we decided on a twenty-minute walk to Notre Dame. The entry line was a block long, but moved along steadily. Once inside, the place was mobbed. It felt like being at the state fair. Hordes of people, shoulder to shoulder, snaked through the cavernous church. The constant sound of voices reminded me of an elementary school at lunch hour.

When navigating the throng proved too much for us, we sat down to rest in front of a statue of Mary. When a man with a long metal stick came along and lit tall candles beside the statue, I suggested that if we sat still something might happen. Sure enough another man began to hand out programs for vespers and I realized we had arrived at the great church on the eve of Pentecost. Before the evening was over we had been through vespers, mass, and a great spectacle, which included the Archbishop of Paris, several dozen priests in red robes, and the confirmation of two hundred adult Catholics.

Though I am not a Catholic, I enjoyed the various liturgies of the church. Hearing the great moaning sounds of the main organ playing the prelude for the confirmation service was a special treat, one that came to me because I gave up and sat down for a while.

My husband, who had never been to Paris before, said he wanted to see the Louvre. I groaned to myself, knowing how huge it is. It feels like miles and miles of galleries. I decided to begin by taking him to see the outside of the building. "There it is," I said as I pointed to the castle turned museum that is large enough to hold an entire college campus. "Which part of it do you want to see?" When we went in the next day, we found the Mona Lisa so Dwight could say he had seen it, then he went off to look at the Dutch Masters and I went off to find my favorite Babylonian statue. The 2,000-year-old statue is a female nude, about ten inches high with ruby eyes, a ruby in her navel, and a gold crescent moon on her head.

First I had to figure out which part of antiquity she was from and which football-stadium-sized wing I should search. It felt like a minor miracle that I hit on the idea of ancient Mesopotamia and found a guide who sent me in the right direction. The Sackler wing, of course. I should have thought of that. After walking for the longest time, I found the statue's case, but she was not there. A terra cotta replica of the statue (along with one of her reclining friend who usually rests beside her) and a small sign explained that she was in the special exhibit on Babylon in the Hall of Napoleon. How many miles away was that!

By then it was an hour before closing time. When I finally located the exhibit back near the main entrance, the gatekeeper said I had to buy a ticket across the lobby. The ticket seller said it was too late because the entrance lines were an hour long. Determined to see the statue, I protested, insisting there was no line at all. I had just been there. A brief consultation with a museum colleague confirmed my claim and I was allowed to purchase a pass.

Babylon, I thought as I crossed the lobby of the Louvre with its unusual glass pyramid overhead. What do I know or care about Babylon? The ancient Israelites were carried into exile there. When I thought really hard I remembered that ancient Babylon was approximately where Iraq is today. A desert, one in which we were currently making a huge mess.

I was not prepared for the beauty of the exhibit or the stunning array of objects from museums in Paris, London, and Berlin—enormous tablets filled with cuneiform writing, gigantic tile terra cotta mosaics of lions, sacred objects of metal and stone. Babylon rose to power after the fall of the Assyrian empire nearly eighteen hundred years before Jesus. Nebuchadnezzar built the Hanging Gardens six hundred years before Christ; three hundred years before Christ the Greeks took control of the area; and near the time of Jesus, an artisan made the small alabaster statue I wanted to see.

I found her in the middle of a large case, surrounded by objects from the same period. She was the most beautiful thing in the exhibit. As I gazed, a little girl walked up to the case and said to her mother, "Look, she has red eyes!"

As with the fine southern art of storytelling, the point of a story is not always the best part. The best part is often the details and the adventures along the way to the point. So it is with a pilgrimage. If you go searching for the holy, you might end up like that small child, amazed to find an alabaster woman with ruby eyes.

Volume 29, Number 2, June 2008

TRACES

I met Katrina Browne ten years ago in California while there visiting friends. A recent graduate of Pacific School of Religion, she described a project she was undertaking. While in seminary she had learned that her family was descended from New England slave traders. Her plan was to retrace the Middle Passage with a group of her relatives. "Good Lord!" I thought. "That's a huge undertaking." I wished her the best of luck.

Ten years later, I received an e-mail saying that Katrina Browne's film, *Traces of the Trade* would air on POV (Point of View) on PBS stations this summer. I almost shrieked with delight at the news. She did it! The documentary premiered at the Sundance Film Festival in January 2008 and was picked up by POV afterwards. I have now seen the film, attended a conference on it, and read a companion book.

Katrina's ancestors, the DeWolfs of Bristol, Rhode Island, were the largest and most successful slave-trading family in Early America. At first she thought they were an aberration, since New England was famous as abolitionist territory. Much to her horror, she learned that the whole town of Bristol was entangled in the slave trade and that the economy of New England was dependent on it. Even after slavery was abolished in northern states, textile mills in the North relied on southern plantations to supply them with cotton grown by enslaved people. That's why she subtitled the film A Story of the Deep North.

The DeWolfs brought over 10,000 people from Africa to the Caribbean and North America in a large, lucrative, and dangerous business. They carried rum from New England to the west coast of Africa where they traded it for Africans. They took the Africans to Cuba or sold them in Charleston, South Carolina. They picked up sugar and molasses in Cuba and took it to New England to make into rum. Before it was all over they owned warehouses, ships, sugar plantations in Cuba, rum distilleries, and the company to insure it all.

This went on for three generations, from 1769 to 1820. Even after importing slaves was illegal in the US, the DeWolfs continued the triangular trade, leaving the Africans in Cuba. Political favors kept US officials from interfering. They were so successful that one DeWolf trader was the second wealthiest man in the US.

Katrina found nine relatives to journey with her from Bristol to Ghana and on to Cuba. Along the way, the family struggled with the meaning of slavery—for them and for white America. The film documents their psychological and geographical journey. Tom DeWolf captured his experience of the journey in *Inheriting the Trade: A Northern Family Confronts Its Legacy as the Largest Slave-Trading Dynasty in U.S. History.*

The Episcopal Diocese of North Carolina held a conference in early September and showed the documentary. Other family members, Dain Perry and his wife Constance, were present to lead a discussion. Unitarians have developed a religious education curriculum to accompany the film. I recommend the film as well as the resources you will find at: www.tracesofthetrade.org.

Volume 29, Number 3, September 2008

OBAMA

For the last few years, whenever a waitperson in a restaurant or a clerk in a store asked, "What would you like," I'd answer, "A new president." Sometimes they'd smile. Sometimes they'd say, "Me too." Very late at night on Tuesday, November 4, 2008, I got what I wanted. I'm so excited that I'm like a teenager with a new rock star. I just want to look at pictures of Barack Obama and watch endless TV interviews with him.

We have elected a president who is not another white guy. This man cares about and is personally related to much of the world. He was born into a multicultural family in a multicultural state, Hawaii. His father was Kenyan and his mother from Kansas was part Irish. (I was delighted to hear a song on YouTube that goes: "O'Leary, O'Riley, O'Hare and O'Hara, there's no one as Irish as Barack Obama.") His half sister, who is half Indonesian, married a man who is Chinese and has a child who is mostly Asian. The president-elect has half siblings who are Kenyan and his wife Michelle has a cousin who is a black rabbi in Chicago. When John Kennedy was elected, we thought being Irish and Catholic was being diverse. This year, Joe Biden's Catholicism was hardly mentioned.

America has often been called the great melting pot, but the white supremacy that has governed much of the land resisted the mixing of light- and dark-skinned people. In the Jim Crow South, interracial marriage was dreaded by many whites and illegal in many southern states.

Now a man who is biracial and talks about it has been elected to the highest office in the land. Very few people I know thought it would really happen. We observe the racism around us on a daily basis and know the racism in our own hearts. Barack Obama would be the last person to suggest that we have solved the problems of racism in this country, the problems of the historical and systemic oppression of people of color. But we've made a powerful symbolic gesture in that direction by electing him and giving him the tools to leverage even more change.

When Harvard's Ron Heifetz gave a lecture at Duke Divinity School this fall, he said the role of a good leader is to manage change well. He went on to explain that many of the changes we experience as monumental are actually quite small. For instance, in the evolutionary process the amount of DNA that had to change to get from a chimpanzee to a human being is less than two percent. A small change that makes a big difference.

When I look at Obama, I see a huge change. But maybe he's not all that different. Like other US presidents, he is well educated and well-spoken. He's a lawyer. That's not new. He went to Harvard. That's not new. He worked as a community organizer before law school, which may be a first, but serving the good of the community is not. His wife is an attorney. Even that's not new. There will be little children in the White House. Again. His mother-in-law will probably move into the White House along with his family. I doubt that's a first.

So, what is different? He looks different. His family tree reaches into a community that may be a first. His mother-in-law, his wife Michelle, and his daughters are descended from proud people in South Carolina who survived being enslaved, people who were brought to these shores against their will and provided much of the labor that built this country. That's different. And that difference, along with more public apologies and more efforts toward restitution, would go a long way toward healing one of the worst collective sins of this nation and one of the most painful divisions among its people.

In many ways, Barack Obama will be like other presidents. He'll be better than many and only time will tell whether he will be considered one of the best. But from the day he was elected he began to send a different message to the world: This is what power and authority look like. This is what the First Family of the USA looks like. If he does nothing else, he has changed the world just by standing there.

Hillary Clinton's presence would have also been a change. No woman has ever occupied the Oval Office. I was surprised that I, as a feminist, was not more enthusiastic about Hillary as a candidate. Many of my friends were. I was enthusiastic about the election of her husband to the

White House and happy when she became a senator from New York. I guess that I was reluctant to go back and that I've never quite forgiven Bill Clinton for not being able to control his appetites. He was a fine president, but his presidency ended badly, and I don't recall that he ever publicly apologized. I wasn't ready to send that whole family back to the White House. I wanted a different family sitting around the breakfast table discussing the future of the world.

Once Barack won the Democratic nomination this summer, I really wanted to see the Obamas up close. First I attended a small event for Michelle in Durham in September and heard her speak. I was impressed by how clear she was that the election was about all of us. I was so excited that when it was my turn to shake her hand, all I could get out of my mouth was, "Thank you, thank you, thank you."

Then I wound up in Asheville on a weekend in early October and learned that Barack was coming to town. I searched the Internet for a place he might show up in addition to the Sunday afternoon stadium event for thousands. I discovered an annual western North Carolina Democratic fundraiser to be held that Saturday night and bought last-minute tickets. A small group of us attended the dinner, as did 700 other hopeful people. Sure enough, between the salad and the main course, Governor Mike Easley got up, mumbled a few sentences, and then announced, "The next President of the United States." The crowd went wild. We were near the back of the ballroom, so I jumped up on my chair and started screaming my head off. Everyone had the same plan. It's a good thing the speech was taped, because all I heard was Senator Obama say, "I hope you don't mind my crashing your party." Who was he kidding? We were thrilled out of our minds.

The speech was over in a flash and for the rest of the evening I kept asking, "Were we really in the same room with Barack Obama?"

The next month was nerve-wracking. My friends were a wreck. They were anxious and no one was sleeping well. I kept remembering Maureen Dowd's advice to Democrats to breathe into a paper bag and stop making plans to move to Canada. I began to think of all the excitement and fear as labor pains. We were birthing a new America. In the last weeks leading up to the election, I kept saying, "It's happening!" We were all in labor:

the contractions, the yelps of pain, the terror (will we come out of this alive?), rumors of dire consequences, claims for certain success.

The campaign in Durham was amazing. People had been organizing, canvassing, and registering new voters since February. In the end, I wound up organizing and feeding volunteers at my neighbor Faulkner's house. She had emerged as the chair of Durham for Obama and, along with her husband Gunther, turned their house into a satellite campaign office. Over the last four days we had nearly 1,000 people come through to get instructions for door knocking, to make last-minute phone calls, and to enter data. It was one of the best volunteer experiences of my life. People were wonderful. They were generous, patient, clear about what they were willing to do, and reliable about doing it. We found tasks for everyone. Leaders emerged for work groups. It was amazing to watch.

Election Day was wet and messy. Volunteers donned slickers and ponchos, got rain-soaked anyway, and kept right on going. When all was said and done, Durham turned in a 70,000-vote lead for Obama and, you could argue, carried the state.

Now, we have a new president, or at least a new president-elect. When waitpeople in restaurants ask me what I want, I just smile and order my food. I have what I want for the moment. I'm willing to give the new administration a few weeks to get organized. It will take a while to undo the culture of deception and greed fostered by the current administration. In the first few days, I expect the new president and his extended family to settle into the White House. I expect Obama to close Guantanamo Bay, end the use of torture, and make a plan to draw down the troops in Iraq. I expect him to create job programs and do whatever government can do to ease the current recession. I expect Congress to pass universal health care for children again and for this president to sign the bill. I expect to have a president who loves us. And I expect all of us to keep working to create the change we seek, to make this a better world for all living creatures. The experience of this fall has given us hope and emboldened us to say, "Yes, we can."

Volume 29, Number 4, December 2008

LABYRINTH

I was glad I had remembered to pack a wool sweater, a hat, and gloves when I went to San Francisco in January of 1997, because it was cold. On a cloudy morning, I dressed warmly and took a cable car from the apartment where I was staying to Grace Cathedral in order to walk their labyrinth. I had fallen so in love with this form of walking meditation at the cathedral the year before that I had vowed to make a labyrinth.

I made good on that promise a few months later at a spirituality retreat I led in western North Carolina. The group and I rolled out newsprint to cover a forty-by-forty-foot space. We then drew a full-sized labyrinth using a pencil, a string, and magic markers. I wasn't even sure it would work. I was afraid the crunching of feet on paper would so distract everyone that no one would enjoy the walk. But the pattern, found in the stone floor of Chartres Cathedral in France, is so compelling that it worked. As people began to make their way through the thirteen concentric circles, they settled into their own interior journeys.

I was looking forward to a journey of my own on that cold January morning as I sat on a pew and waited for the right moment to start my walk. Several rows of pews had been removed from the back of the church to make room for the Grace Cathedral carpet labyrinth, which is open to the public when the church is open. I sat and watched light streaming through high stained-glass windows and resting on the labyrinth. Only a man in a red jacket, a woman in gray socks, and one other man were walking.

I stared at the pattern, trying to follow the path with my eyes. The labyrinth at Grace is a forty-foot circle containing a winding path that leads from the outer edge to the center. The design came from Chartres Cathedral in France where it was laid into the floor in the thirteenth century. A labyrinth has no dead ends or tricks. By following the path, a walker eventually reaches the center. The path is just complicated enough to prevent a walker from knowing how far it is to the beginning or the end. Eventually my mind gives up wondering and gives over to just following the walking.

When the time felt right, I took off my shoes and stepped onto the purple and gray carpeted path. I walked slowly, paying attention to my steps and my thoughts and feelings, rounding the curves until I reached the center and its six-petaled rose. I walked across the center to the petal that pointed toward the altar.

As I stood there, my feet were awash in red light, my mid-section in lavender, and my head in the warm golden light of the sun. I stood very still, soaking in the light as though I were soaking in the love of the sun or the love of God the Creator. Then I sat down and watched as the red light moved slowly across the center of the labyrinth, like the Holy Spirit floating through the middle of our lives.

I looked up to see which window was throwing all these beautiful colors on the labyrinth and was startled to see an image of a printing press. Publishing! It seemed like a sign, like a Western Union telegram from God saying, "Write!" I could have come on any day in any season and I wound up there on the day when the window with the words, "The words will stand forever" and an image of the Gutenberg Press threw a rainbow of light right on me.

As I sat there with tongues of fire lapping at my feet, I nearly burst into tears. "But I can't write," I wanted to wail. "I don't have anything to say. No one will listen to me." But a voice inside insisted, "When God says write, you write. When the creative force in the universe says speak, you speak." I was already writing almost every day, I just didn't have any confidence in what I was doing.

The light moved. I moved one petal to the north, and the light lined up in front of me. I was facing due south with southern light streaming in on me. The southland was calling me home; that much seemed clear. I said a silent prayer that I might be as brave about writing and publishing as I had been about making my first labyrinth.

I got up, left the center, and retraced my steps to the opening at the edge of the labyrinth. Then I sat down again on the back pew. As I rested and made notes in my journal, an icon of Mary Magdalene caught my eye. I thanked Mary Magdalene for being an alternative image of woman. For being one of the disciples. For possibly being Jesus' lover or partner, certainly for being Jesus' friend. Then I lit a candle for my friends and myself, for women who were a little different, women who wanted to make things, to write, to follow their hearts.

That was a dozen years ago. In the summer of 1997, friends and I constructed a full-sized canvas labyrinth. Since then several thousand people have walked our labyrinth. When two of the panels were inadvertently damaged by a dry cleaner, friends helped draw and paint the replacements.

RCWMS has led dozens of labyrinth walks, workshops, and programs. Walking the labyrinth can be a good way of centering oneself. The serpentine path provides a metaphor for life's journey. Walking can be a time to open the heart, to experience the presence of the holy, to attend to life's questions. Often when I walk the labyrinth, I get more clarity about my life or a possible solution to a problem.

It takes thirty minutes to an hour for a person to walk the labyrinth. In an hour and a half, twenty to thirty people can walk and have a little time afterwards for individual reflection. A three-hour workshop provides enough time for an introduction, walking, journaling, and group discussion. An all-day workshop can include several times for walking, guided meditation, simple art projects, and journaling.

To schedule a labyrinth program or workshop or for more information, contact the Resource Center at rcwmsnc@aol.com.

Volume 30, Number 1, March 2009

MEINRAD

When Amy Kellum attended visionary artist Meinrad Craighead's slide lecture at Duke University in 1999, her understanding of God got bigger, a lot bigger. It exploded, making room for the feminine divine. She signed up for a workshop at Meinrad's studio in Albuquerque, and that did it. Amy was hooked. The next time Meinrad lectured in Durham, Amy chauffeured her around and asked, "What are you going to do with those slides?" "I'm leaving them to someone in my will," Meinrad answered. "No," Amy persisted, "what are you going to do with them now?" "Oh, you can do something with them if you want to. I'm tired. Can we talk about this tomorrow?"

Tomorrow turned into years as Amy figured out how to preserve Meinrad's work and share her message. She bought a video camera, enrolled in Duke's Center for Documentary Studies, and filmed Meinrad's lectures around the country. She made a ten-minute film about Meinrad (see www.meinradproject.org/about). When she wondered what to do next, I suggested she make an hour-long PBS-quality documentary. "How do I do that?" Amy asked. The answer was easy: the Minnow gals.

Donna Campbell and Georgann Eubanks of Minnow Media said they'd be happy to work on a film about Meinrad and that it would cost $100,000. Amy and I almost fainted, but she got right on it. Amy created the Meinrad Craighead Documentary Project at RCWMS and began her main job as the Executive Producer of *Meinrad Craighead: Praying with Images*—raising money.

Amy's friend Becky Carver made the first gift in April 2005. Four years, 500 donors, and $120,000 later, the film is finished! In four years, Amy made seven trips to New Mexico, attended Meinrad's lectures in four US cities, and accompanied the artist to Paris, Florence, Rome, and Barcelona. The film crew went to New Mexico twice and interviewed twenty people. Georgann wrote a brilliant script capturing the essence of Meinrad's life and work, Donna edited hours of tape into a fabulous film.

The first public screening was Thursday, May 21, 7:00 p.m., at the Nasher Museum at Duke. We chose the Nasher because of its elegant environment and exquisite sound and projection system, but Amy worried we'd run out of seats. The auditorium only holds 190. At 6:45 there were still empty seats, but then people started pouring in. We knew the Nasher wouldn't let anyone stand.

With Meinrad sitting in the front row, Amy and I stepped up to the mic, Amy looking happier than I had ever seen her. I began, "Welcome, and some of you will have to leave the room." After the opening, I ran out to see if I could help with the extra people. The Nasher opened two overflow rooms and 263 people got to see the film. When I returned to the darkened auditorium and sat down on the back row, I leaned my head back against the wall and breathed a sigh of relief. I looked up at the screen and could not believe my eyes. The images were large and luscious, image after image of Meinrad's work. The narration was compelling in Courtney Reid-Eaton's reassuring voice and Meinrad's quotes were read soulfully by Randa McNamara. It was astonishing.

It worked! People came. The film was gorgeous and Meinrad had a good time. What a night!

Volume 30, Number 2, June 2009

TIBBIE

I've known Tibbie Roberts since the late 1970s when, just out of seminary, I joined the North Carolina Council of Churches Committee for the Equal Rights Amendment of which she was a member. Older than my mother, she was one of the sturdy United Methodist women who kept the committee going.

When I saw Tibbie at a meeting last winter, she proudly announced she was ninety-four years old. As bright and energetic as ever, she claimed to have driven herself the three hours from Morehead City to Raleigh that day. Seeing her made me wonder whether her papers had been archived, so I called her soon after and asked. She was interested, so I got her in touch with Laura Micham at the Sallie Bingham Center for Women's History and Culture at Duke (which houses RCWMS's papers). Since I was going to the coast in February for our art workshop, I arranged to pick up some of Tibbie's papers in Morehead City. Amelia Stinson-Wesley, who was on the Equal Rights committee in its later years, wanted to go along—to the workshop and most of all to see Tibbie.

When Amelia and I arrived at Tibbie's house that bright February morning, she had piles of papers and photographs all laid out for us. Instead of just loading them into the car, however, she wanted to tell us about them, so we spent a couple of hours going through the many and varied committees, events, and trips represented. I knew Tibbie was amazing but had no idea she had been involved in so many things.

Tibbie Roberts was often present when history was made and had papers, pictures, and tote bags to prove it. She was elected as a delegate from North Carolina to the National Women's Conference in Houston in 1977. Over 20,000 people gathered to celebrate International Women's Year and identify goals for women for the next decade.

In the late 1970s, the North Carolina Council of Churches asked Tibbie to coordinate a statewide campaign to increase the religious support for the ERA. While Tibbie was considering this request, her Aunt Lena found something Tibbie's grandmother, Laura Nelson Duncan, had written in 1878 while a student at Greensboro College. Entitled "Turnabout is Fair Play," the piece began, "Move over you liege lords, and let the ladies show you what they can do!" Tibbie said that was all the encouragement she needed. She wrote the Council of Churches saying that her grandmother had spoken from the grave and that she'd take the job.

After the ERA failed, the North Carolina Council of Churches committee became the Equal Rights Committee and kept going for another twenty years, Tibbie right along with it. She participated in the North Carolina Council for Women and is still a member of The Women's Forum of North Carolina.

She served two terms on the United Methodist General Board of Global Ministries (GBGM) and was their representative to the Interfaith Center on Corporate Responsibility. She represented ICCR at an AT&T shareholders meeting in the late 1980s. She traveled as a representative of the GBGM to China, Israel/Palestine, and to at least one country in Africa. She has been out of the country more than twenty times.

She was President of United Methodist Women (UMW), of the North Carolina Conference (eastern North Carolina) when the controversial Re-Imagining Conference took place in Minneapolis in 1993. Sponsored by the World Council of Churches as part of its Decade of Churches in Solidarity with Women, the conference was supported by national United Methodist funds. Tibbie sent a UMW delegate and took a lot of heat after the conference when conservative publicity painted the feminist gathering as heretical and pagan. She stood by her decision and supported her delegate.

She attended the UN's Fourth World Conference on Women in Beijing in September 1995, whose theme was "Look at the World Through Women's Eyes." She went back to Beijing for a follow-up conference in 1999.

After going through the papers and loading them into the trunk of my car, Tibbie took us to lunch in her native Beaufort, just across the river. Tibbie's family in Beaufort goes way back to the 1700s, so after lunch we had a guided tour. Next she wanted to go to an art show, so we drove to the other end of town for that. Amelia and I dropped Tibbie back at her house mid-afternoon. Though we had planned to stop at the aquarium afterwards, we were too tired. Tibbie had worn us out, but we came away with a great idea—to have a ninty-fifth birthday party for her close to her birthday on June 2.

The secret of Tibbie's health and strength may be that she still goes to Curves three times a week. Or it might be how much she loves living and loves the people in her life. She raised four daughters, three of whom still live nearby and came to the birthday lunch in Raleigh. They enjoy their mother so much that they often take vacations with her.

I don't think I've ever seen Tibbie Roberts without her head in a scarf. She must have a huge collection of them, because they always match what she has on. At ninety-five her hair is still coal black, though I suspect she helps its color along. I'm not sure if it is still long, but it used to be really long, and she wore it wound up on top of her head. The scarf, with a wave of black hair peeking out, is a striking look. Dramatic.

She wore a bright green scarf the day thirteen of us met for birthday lunch at The Irregardless Cafe in Raleigh. Several others wanted to attend but couldn't. Amelia had gall bladder surgery. Former Equal Rights Committee members Bett Hargrave and Doris Morrison were home recuperating, Bett from a knee replacement and Doris from an injured foot. Mildred Fry, who is almost as old as Tibbie, was present, along with George Reed (director of the North Carolina Council of Churches), Jean Rodenbough (the Council's new president), and more. We had a wonderful time.

The day Amelia and I were at Tibbie's house, I asked her if she was the oldest person in Morehead City who was still active. She paused a moment and said with a big smile, "I believe I am."

Volume 30, Number 2, June 2009

PAULI

Face Up!—a mural project sponsored by Duke's Center for Documentary Studies—brought Brett Cooke to Durham in 2008 to create a dozen murals around town. Six of them depict Pauli Murray. Putting her image on the TROSA building across from the YMCA and on the old Durham Food Coop on Chapel Hill Street got people talking about this remarkable woman.

Murray was born November 20, 1911, and died July 1, 1985. After her mother died, four-year-old Pauli went to Durham, North Carolina, to live with her maternal grandparents, the Fitzgeralds, and her mother's sisters, Pauline and Sally, in a house on what is now Carroll Street. Though born in Baltimore, she graduated from high school in Durham, and Durham claims her as a daughter.

Today, when anyone in Durham says "Pauli Murray," people come. Durham Public Library sponsored a panel about Pauli Murray last winter, and a crowd showed up on a miserable rainy afternoon. Local Episcopal churches sponsored a convocation in Murray's honor at St. Titus Episcopal Church in July, and so many people came that they ran out of seats. The same churches sponsored a discussion of Murray's *Proud Shoes* in August and sixty-five people came. To a book discussion in August!

People seem hungry to discuss the issues raised by this lawyer, scholar, poet, and priest and her tireless efforts on behalf of civil rights and women's rights. Murray was arrested in 1940 in Virginia for refusing to sit at the back of a bus. Later she researched laws on race in the South and published *States' Laws on Race and Color*. She cofounded the National Organization for Women (NOW). Her story provides an opportunity to explore the complexity of our communities. With her multiple ancestries (African, European, and Native American), Murray insisted she was neither this nor that. She understood herself to be black and white, slave and free, male and female.

114

Several upcoming efforts will focus on Murray. The Duke Center for Human Rights created the Pauli Murray Project, directed by Barbara Lau (balau@duke.edu), to educate the community about Murray and promote the values for which she stood. For Murray's centennial next year, RCWMS will sponsor an art exhibit at St. Philip's Episcopal Church in Durham. The Episcopal Diocese of North Carolina nominated Murray for inclusion in Lesser Feasts and Fasts, their version of the list of saints.

That afternoon at the Chapel of the Cross, in 1977, the congregation sang, "In Christ there is no East or West, in him no South or North, but one great fellowship of love throughout the whole wide earth." That's the kind of world Pauli Murray worked for all her life.

Volume 30, Number 3, September 2009

WORDS

I sometimes wonder to myself, "How many words could a writer write if a writer would write words?" One day recently, I wrote for almost two hours in the morning, an hour or more in the afternoon, and then I edited for two hours that night. The next day, I said something about this to Liz Dowling-Sendor, our new Writer in Residence at RCWMS. Liz was once a journalist, so I told her that I don't see how reporters do it, write all day, and she said, "They don't." She said that two hours a day of writing was about all most humans could manage. I was surprised. I had been feeling like a total wimp, a fraud, because I could only manage an hour, or two tops, on the mornings I set aside for writing. Here's why.

A few years ago, I heard an author named Jane Yolen read at a local bookstore. She has published over 170 books, many of them wonderful historical fiction for young people. In the Q&A, I asked a question I often ask writers, "How do you get your work done? How are your days structured?" Yolen said that she writes for eight to ten hours a day. Maybe I heard her wrong. Maybe she said she works for eight to ten hours a day, spending some hours on correspondence or finances. Whatever she does, it works, and she has all those books to show for it. I have felt like a fake ever since.

In *Bird by Bird*, Annie Lamott says that if you write 300 words a day, in a year you will have written a book. That's even with time out for birthdays, Christmas, and going to the doctor. Three hundred words is about one page, double spaced. I thought she meant, "Any dummy can write 300 words a day." I took her at her word and started writing 300 words a day in my computer. That was fourteen or fifteen years ago. But those files rarely turn into a book. Well, OK, once, they became a book. The entries in 1997 and 1998 became *Hurricane Season*. But they become other things, like articles for this newsletter. I rearranged my life so that I write in the mornings, and I am very strict about my mornings. No appointments. No work for RCWMS. No e-mail. (OK,

I cheat on that all the time!) Nothing, except sometimes swimming, walking, or a writing group once a month. But that's all.

I rearranged my life to write. And I do it. And I'm really slow. But I have published books. For me, writing is all about making the time to do it. I have started a new writing practice with Liz. We call it TWT (trapped writing time). I'm at my computer and she's at hers. We pick a starting time, show up at our computers, and e-mail each other, saying "OK go!" Then we write for forty-five minutes, or until we can't stand it any more, and then e-mail, "How are you doing?" We like to say that TWT is a B.I.T.C.H., which stands for "Butt In The Chair, Honey." Without sitting down to the writing, writing never happens.

So I guess the question is, "How many words could a writer write if a writer would sit down?" Keep your pen moving or your fingers on the keyboard. Until we figure out how to get the words to go straight from our brains and to the page, we will simply have to sit down and write.

Volume 30, Number 3, September 2009

TEAHOUSE

It was raining the September morning I had agreed to join my friend Dot Borden for a traditional Japanese tea gathering in the teahouse in Duke Gardens. As I grabbed my raincoat and umbrella, I wondered about the advisability of attending anything in a building with paper walls in the rain. Since I stay home in the mornings to write, I was surprised I had agreed to go. Clearly, I wanted to take part in the event.

I became interested in Japan when I was a child. My doctor father was drafted into the Air Force during the Korean War in the early 1950s. Afterwards, he volunteered for the Tulsa Air National Guard and began traveling on military air transport (MATS) planes to Hawaii and Japan, just because he could. He built a small Japanese garden at our house, adding soft grass, bamboo, a low bench, steppingstones, and a stone lantern. He hung a painted scroll at the end of a long hall inside. When he moved into a new medical office, he had shoji screens built and pasted fake Japanese characters onto the chart holders outside the examining rooms.

In 1960, Daddy took Mother and me to Hawaii. On the way, we stopped in San Francisco and visited the gorgeous Japanese Garden at Golden Gate Park. The next year, we went to Japan. Americans were still a novelty, and dark-headed school children in matching uniforms stopped us on the Ginza to practice their English. We visited the Golden Pavilion in Kyoto. I was nipped in the butt by a deer at the Deer Park in Nara. And we rode the fast train through the countryside. I've been fascinated by all things Japanese ever since.

When Dot suggested the tea gathering, I was delighted. I had attended a Japanese tea while I was in college, led by the wife of my professor of Buddhism. She had studied tea in Japan while he studied religion. I wanted to attend a tea gathering again and wanted to spend some time in the new teahouse in the Duke Gardens.

118

The teahouse was built as part of the Durham Sister Cities Program, which pairs Durham with four cities around the world, including Toyama, Japan. Volunteers had worked for twenty years to develop relationships and raise money before undertaking the construction of the teahouse. Dot Borden, the program's founder, served for many years as board president.

When I arrived at the gardens and realized there would be only eight guests for tea, I felt as though I had won a contest. I was lucky to be part of this special event.

We walked through the soft mist to the entrance of the tea garden, surrounded by a graceful wooden fence. Once inside the garden, our host Mr. Nakasone poured water into a large ceramic bowl in which we would purify our hands before entering the teahouse. Mr. Nakasone, a landscape architect and tea master from Toyama, was invited to Durham to teach garden design and conduct tea gatherings.

Each of the objects and gestures that are part of the ceremony has beauty and purpose and helps to focus the mind. I gazed into the beautiful basin as I lifted the wooden dipper, poured water first over my left hand, then over my right, and then let the water dribble down the handle to cleanse the dipper itself.

Leaving umbrellas, coats, and shoes outside, we entered the teahouse through a square door less than three feet high, a door I had mistaken for a pass-through for items used in the tea. Entering through the low door is said to make everyone the same, as differences in status or wealth fall away.

Inside, a scroll and flower arrangement adorned an alcove on one side of the tiny room. Shoji screens formed two sides of the room and wooden walls the other two. We sat on the floor on tatami mats or in chairs and waited for our host to enter. Each time he entered or left the room, he knelt and opened the sliding shoji screen by moving it first with one hand and then the other. I was aware that every gesture had evolved over the centuries and had been repeated thousands of times.

I watched as Mr. Nakasone served sweets on a tray shaped like the region of Toyama. I listened for the sound of the water when he removed the lid of the iron pot, raised the steaming liquid with a bamboo ladle, and poured it back into the pot. I watched as he scooped powdered green tea with a small curved bamboo implement and placed it into a beautiful raku tea bowl. He added water, whisked the tea, and served it to the first guest.

Nancy Hamilton, a local tea leader, instructed us about when to bow, when to lift the tea bowl with the right hand, place it on the left palm, turn it 180 degrees, and drink the frothy green brew. The bitter taste was jarring in the quiet setting, and I was glad I had saved part of my sweets to eat after drinking my tea.

Though I sit fairly comfortably on the floor, I got fidgety, readjusting my legs when an ankle or foot began to ache. I tried to hold still and admire the mats on the floor, the simple graceful implements, and the damp beauty visible just outside each time our host opened the door.

It was beautiful and moving to sit in that peaceful setting and participate in a centuries-old practice with a master who spoke not a word of English. I felt as satisfied as I had on my first visit to the Japanese Garden at Golden Gate Park nearly fifty years before. I had been searching all those years for a fleeting beauty that finally found me again in a teahouse in Durham.

At the end of the tea, Nancy taught us to say, "Arigato" (thank you). Before I left, I used the one bit of language I remembered from my childhood visit to Japan. I pulled out my tiny red Canon camera, turned to our host and the women who had helped him, said, "Ichi, ni, san," (one, two, three), and snapped a picture. Walking back across the gardens to the parking lot, I felt as though I were returning from a trip to a far-off land. If Dot Borden worked all those years to bring Durham and Toyama closer together, she had certainly succeeded that day.

Volume 30, Number 4, December 2009

UPDATE

The Duke Divinity Women's Center honored Jill Raitt at its 35th Anniversary Celebration last November. Jill was the first woman on the Divinity School faculty and she kindly gave up her office in the school's basement so the newly founded center could have a home in the fall of 1974. At the anniversary celebration, Therese Berger, now of Yale Divinity School, gave the first Jill Raitt Lecture. Those attending included former students Nancy Rosebaugh, Joann Abel, Linda Hawkins, Fran Olson, Jenny Graves, Helen Neinast, Amelia Stinson-Wesley, Rosanna Panizo, Betty Wolfe, Ron Moss, and Carol Burnett, and friends such as Lois MacGillivray, Betsy Alden, Jean O'Barr, Sarah Freedman, Lori Pistor, and Laurie Hays Coffman. I served as the second director of the Women's Center and was part of the planning committee along with current Women's Center co-coordinators Brandy Daniels and Emma Akpan, RCWMS intern Meghan Florian, and Divinity Professor Mary McClintock Fulkerson.

Since the first of the year, RCWMS has hosted two writing weeks at the beach as well as an art workshop. I've been up and down the road to the coast a lot, but I can't complain. It's a treat to go to the beach and be with wonderful women. When I drove over the bridge to Emerald Isle, North Carolina, in mid-February at about 6:00 p.m., the sun had just set and the western horizon was flushed with a deep pink. I glanced at the water that separates Emerald Isle from the mainland and noticed that each of the small grassy islands in the sound was surrounded by a pink glow. I looked again and decided it must be low tide. Wet sand around each island was reflecting the sky.

That color was a wonderful welcome to Finding Your Medium, our art workshop with Sue Sneddon. In addition to Sue's inspiring teaching, a highlight of the weekend was her beach encounter with a live seal. When we contacted a North Carolina marine biologist, we learned that our waters do have seals, that they should be left alone to rest on the beach, and that they have teeth.

FILMS

Our newest documentary *Blackbirds, Bottle Caps, & Broken Records: Environmental Artist Bryant Holsenbeck at Work* was shown in January as part of Strange Beauty, a film festival in Durham, North Carolina. Filmmaker Margaret Morales came from Miami, Florida, for the event and the film team (Margaret, Bryant, Jenny Graves, and I) was able to have one more delicious evening together. Jenny had just moved back from a semester in Philadelphia. She is now working as a community organizer for Clean Energy Durham. Margaret has a similar job in Miami working on clean water. To order the film ($15 includes tax and postage), send a check to RCWMS, 1202 Watts Street, Durham, NC 27701 or go to www.rwcms.org.

Our hour-long documentary *Meinrad Craighead: Praying with Images* will be shown at two locations in California in March. Join Executive Producer Amy Kellum for a public screening at Ebenezer/herchurch Lutheran in San Francisco on Monday, March 22 at 7:00 p.m. or First Congregational Church of Berkeley on Tuesday, March 23 at 7:00. The screenings are free and open to the public. The DVD may be ordered for $35 (includes tax and postage). Send a check to RCWMS, 1202 Watts Street, Durham, NC 27701 or go to www.meinradproject.org.

Volume 31, Number 1, March 2010

75TH ANNIVERSARY

The North Carolina Council of Churches was founded in 1935 by H. Shelton Smith, a theology professor at Duke Divinity School. I heard about this crusader for ecumenism and racial justice when I was in seminary at Duke. Smith was long retired by then, but a Duke friend, Susan Brooks Thistlethwaite, was researching his career.

Seventy-five years later, this May, friends and supporters of the Council gathered at Duke Divinity School to celebrate the work, witness, and people of the council. I appreciated Dr. Richard Smith's recollections of his father. He told one moving story about a dreadful event in Durham. When Richard was about eleven, a white bus driver shot a black man in the back and killed him. H. Shelton Smith took his son with him to the trial. When the not guilty verdict was returned, Richard recalls that the judge put his head down on the bench. Afterwards the father took his son back to the judge's chambers and asked, "Why did you put your head down when the verdict was announced?" According to Richard, the judge replied he was considering declaring a mistrial for this gross miscarriage of justice.

Other speakers noted the council's work on gender equity, migrant farmworkers, North Carolina's tobacco economy, the death penalty, and GLBT (gay, lesbian, bisexual, and transgendered) issues. The beloved name of Sr. Evelyn Mattern was invoked again and again. Evelyn served two stints as a social justice officer for the council and staffed the Equal Rights Committee.

I enjoyed Bett Hargrave's account of the North Carolina Council of Churches' Equal Rights Committee, which would not stop meeting after the ERA was defeated in 1982. I was fortunate to serve on the committee as it carried on for another twenty years. The group's last effort, led by Sr. Evelyn, was a theater piece on women in the religious community in North Carolina, *The Women's Coffeehouse of Spirit*.

My favorite part was seeing friends, especially Jean Rodenbough, current President of the Council; Brigit Johnson, former Council President; former staff, Collins Kilburn and Jimmy Creech; and the elder feminists: Julia Elsie, B. Holt and Tibbie Roberts. Julia (only in her eighties) has worked long years on behalf of migrant workers. B. Holt (nearly ninety-four) served as a state legislator from Alamance County for many years, and Tibbie is still active at the tender age of ninety-six.

During the evening worship, I sat on a row with Tibbie, Julia, Bett, and B. We listened to Jean Rodenbough's words of welcome and were inspired by the clear vision of Hope Morgan Ward, Bishop of the Mississippi Conference of the United Methodist Church. Hope reminded us that the Ecumenical movement started with a conference in Edinburgh in 1910. She noted that the North Carolina Council of Churches was almost the only integrated assembly in North Carolina in the 1950s. She reminded us that God is in every place where the dignity of life is threatened, where injustice holds sway. She inspired us to stay in the world, to continue the good work, to keep the faith.

Listening to the bishop, I remembered Helen Crotwell, former Associate Minister at Duke University and the first woman to run for Bishop in the Southeastern Jurisdiction of the United Methodist Church. Helen didn't win that election, but she paved the way for other women.

Volume 31, Number 2, June 2010

CHOCOLATE

I went to Paris for a week in May and came home raving about two things: chocolate and irises.

On the first morning in Paris, I woke at 5:30 a.m. and went out for a walk. I walked the three or four long blocks to the Seine and crossed a bridge to the Tuileries, but the elaborate iron gates were locked. I walked a little further to a café near the corner of the garden and sat down. After a breakfast of juice, hot cocoa, and a croissant, the garden opened and I strolled in.

There were hardly any people in the garden at 7:00 a.m., a few walking or jogging through, and no one sitting around the large reflecting pool. Empty green metal chairs rested in a random pattern around the edge of the pool. I selected a chair and sat down.

Whoa! I thought as I sat. How do you sit in this thing? The back tilted permanently backward at a forty-five-degree angle; they were soldered on that way. An American recliner would have offered a choice, but not this chair. There was no option but to lean back and relax, open myself to the sky and watch the world at my feet. So I did. What a novel idea for a chair! Being short, I could rest my head on the top edge of the back and recline. A person could go to sleep. It was easily more comfortable than the airplane seat I had occupied a day or so before.

Imagine, chairs in a public park that encouraged lounging and sleeping! Dozens of them.

The next morning, I talked my husband into having breakfast at a café with me. I had picked out a nice-looking one on the Boulevard Saint-Germain, Café de Flore, without knowing that it was once the hang out of Jean Paul Sartre and his crowd. I just wanted a place to sit, eat, and watch all the people in black walk by.

We selected a table on the sidewalk and I sat down facing the street. My husband sat across from me, as we would in any American restaurant, but it wasn't long before the waiter in the long white apron had rearranged us so we were side by side, looking out. That's when I noticed that nearly everyone in the place was facing the street.

When the waiter came back, I ordered orange juice, hot chocolate, and pain au chocolat (a croissant with chocolate inside.) My husband, now on my right, ordered coffee and eggs with ham. And then we waited.

In America, this breakfast outing might have taken all of twenty minutes—to order, get the food, and eat—but in Paris it was closer to an hour and twenty minutes. I was thrilled. The café was not full. No one was in a hurry. Eventually the waiter brought our food and laid a small bill on the table.

In Paris, people aren't paying just for food in a restaurant. They are renting a place to live for a while. I noticed at lunches and dinners over the course of the week that no one ever brought us a check until we asked for it, even after the coffee and dessert were consumed and the last of the dishes cleared away. I concluded that to bring the check would be to suggest that the establishment wanted us to leave, and that would have been rude.

When our breakfast finally arrived, everything at the perfect temperature, I had slowed down enough to be able to taste the food. As I sipped my hot chocolate and ate my bread, the flavors and textures filled me with delight.

When I told this story later, friends commented that they did not know I ate that much chocolate. I don't, or at least I didn't used to. I'm a finicky health food—not too much sugar, chocolate might keep me awake—sort of eater. But I said to myself, "I'm in Paris. Eat!" And so I did.

That's when it happened. I don't know if it was the dark chocolate, the butter in the bread, the whole milk (or was it cream?) in the hot chocolate, but my mouth and body were filled with the taste and the feeling of…of being loved. Of being cared for, of being held, enwrapped, encircled, of falling into a feather bed.

"God, this is good!" I kept thinking to myself. The hot chocolate was not too sweet and not too bitter and went down like silk, and the pain au chocolat was perfect, crisp and buttery with small squeezes of chocolate inside.

"Why does chocolate taste so much better in France?" I kept asking once I returned to the States. Some said, "I'm not sure it does," but I had never ever enjoyed anything quite so much. Perhaps it was the jet lag. Perhaps is was the ceremony—the waiter in black and white, looking like a penguin, speaking both French and English, the small round table with its placemat that fit perfectly inside the rim. Perhaps it was the astronomical price of the food, the stylish people on the street, or the beautiful French man in the white shirt sitting across from us. But I suspect it was the quality of the ingredients and the slow speed at which they were consumed that allowed my whole body to enjoy the experience.

To repeat the experience would cost thousands of dollars and require staying up all night and suffering jet lag for a week. I may do it again, but for now, I am happy I was present enough to enjoy the moment.

Volume 31, Number 3, September 2010

PAULI MURRAY

It has taken me almost a lifetime to discover that true emancipation lies in the acceptance of the whole past, in deriving strength from all my roots, in facing up to the degradation as well as the dignity of my ancestors.
                                        —Pauli Murray, *Proud Shoes*

The Rev. Dr. Pauline (Pauli) Murray was born in Baltimore, Maryland, November 20, 1910, and grew up with relatives in Durham, North Carolina. She completed undergraduate studies at New York's Hunter College, but was denied admission to the University of North Carolina Graduate School because of her race. She graduated top of her class from Howard Law School, the first female to do so. For her predecessors, this had meant a post-graduate fellowship at Harvard, but Harvard refused to admit her because she was a woman. A founding member of the National Organization for Women, Murray worked as a civil rights lawyer, professor, college vice president, writer, adviser to First Lady Eleanor Roosevelt, and deputy attorney general of California. In 1977, Murray became the first black woman in the US to become an Episcopal priest.

Murray's grandmother was the daughter of a white plantation heir and a woman enslaved to his family. Her grandfather was a mixed race Northerner who came to Durham as a teacher determined to lift African Americans out of ignorance and poverty. Murray's autobiography, *Proud Shoes: The Story of an American Family*, chronicles not only her childhood in Durham, but also the early history of Durham as a place in large part built by former slaves, freed blacks, and working class whites.

For more information about Pauli Murray, read her memoir, *Song in a Weary Throat*, Google her, or see: paulimurrayproject.org.

Volume 31, Number 3, September 2010

WHERE AM I NOW?

Where am I now? Where are we now?

I am not an evangelist for Christianity. I am an evangelist for finding or creating a community of support and practices that sustain you. For my beloved Presbyterian grandmother, spiritual support came in reading the Bible and praying every day. For me it comes from a weekly yoga class, from painting and walking, from writing every day, and from feminists with whom I share the journey of faith.

As a writer, I am accustomed to having words and images pour out of me. I am interested in many things feminist, Presbyterian, in ministry, spirituality, creativity, in justice and social change. When asked to write about Christianity these days, I freeze up. Having said that, I acknowledge I am a thoroughgoing Christian—soaked in it, professed in it, ordained in it, and in "good standing" with one arm of it.

Instead of being an apologist, trying to explain Christianity to feminists and feminism to Christians, I choose to be a heretic, to remain within the bounds of the Christian faith, to create new forms, and to explore new practices.

I spend a lot of time with women who grew up as practicing Christians and now have found other, more sustaining practices. Many of them have "defected in place" and some of them simply defected. These deeply spiritual and ethical women would rather do yoga or art than attend a church, even a progressive one, on a Sunday morning. Most of the churches in our area are still Christocentric and use patriarchal language. Some of my feminist colleagues have turned in their ordinations. I have no instinct to do that. I still love the religion of my childhood; it is just that when I step into it these days, I tend to freeze. I do not want to say some of the words anymore.

Almost all the gatherings I am part of are interfaith or multifaith. RCWMS's gatherings may include a Protestant woman who attends a local synagogue and teaches Buddhist dharma, an African American who grew up Protestant and is now a Zen priest, Jewish women who practice Buddhism or yoga, and women who have no interest in claiming any particular religious tradition. The faithful, spiritual feminism I see, organize, and participate in, can hardly be contained in the label "Christian."

I am tired of the ways Christianity has said to people, not just women, "Believe like this, make art like this, make love like this." I have trouble with traditional Christian theology and practice—from baptism, which we cheerfully say is a sign of welcoming a child into a community of faith, but is really the washing away of the uncleanness of being born of a woman; to communion, which can be seen as sharing the feast of the "kingdom," but manages to steal some of the grace from the Passover feast and from food women have prepared at home for thousands of years.

I do not believe in and I cannot subscribe to a version of Christianity that insists that what Jesus meant was that we were to get together regularly and celebrate his torture and murder at the hand of the state. It is misguided theology. It would be like getting together every January 15 and celebrating the cold-blooded murder of Martin Luther King Jr. and saying how fabulous it was that he was murdered in the name of freedom. But maybe that is what we do and in so doing we encourage other people to go get themselves killed for what they believe in.

No thoroughgoing feminist would tolerate the language of torture and violence anymore. Christianity has changed because of a feminist analysis. One stellar example of a new feminist Christianity is found in the work of Rita Nakashima Brock and Rebecca Parker in *Saving Paradise: How Christianity Traded Love of This World for Crucifixion and Empire*. The authors discovered within the early church a Christian esthetic that focused on beauty. They found that in the first thousand years or so of Christianity the focus was on this world as paradise. The focus on Jesus' suffering and dying did not come until Charlemagne forced Europeans to convert at sword point. When the Holy Roman Emperor caused suffering in the name of Christ, it became holy to suffer.

Though feminist Christianity is my spiritual home, my life and work have carried me beyond, outside, and around the corner from exclusive Christianity. My perspective is certainly not feminist Judaism, or feminist Buddhism, or even secular feminism, but the weddings, funerals, naming ceremonies, workshops, retreats, and writing I am involved in no longer take an exclusively Christian view. They are much closer to the ground, to the seasons and cycles, to things that my inherited Christianity was trying to squelch.

Do not get me wrong. I actually love Jesus. I just have a really hard time with how the church has so often screwed up his message of liberation and wholeness, his concern for every person, his love of justice, his practice of peace. But I do not think he is the only one or the only way. Christianity is the path my ancestors left me. I am stuck being a Southerner (which I like just fine), being white (which is something of a burden in this country), being female (which is great), and being Christian (which I claim but have no interest in defending), and increasingly interfaith. I do not need or want to be with people of faith who are only like me. Being in a gathering with only Christians is as boring as being in a gathering of only white people, unless the conversation is about how we have used our position to limit ourselves and oppress other people. Feminist Christianity invites so much more than that.

Note: "Where Am I Now?" by Jeanette Stokes is taken from an essay in *New Feminist Christianity: Many Voices, Many Views*, edited by Mary E. Hunt and Diane L. Neu (Woodstock, VT: SkyLight Paths Publishing, 2010). Permission granted by SkyLight Paths Publishing, P.O. Box 237, Woodstock, VT 05091, www.skylightpaths.com.

Volume 31, Number 3, September 2010

THREADS

On Friday evening, November 19, several hundred people passed through St. Philip's Episcopal Church in Durham. As they ate, drank, and chatted with one another, they admired and remarked on the amazing quilts and other textile art in the hallways of the church. The exhibit that delighted so many that evening, "Strength from All My Roots," was organized by RCWMS in honor of the centennial of the Rev. Dr. Pauline (Pauli) Murray. RCWMS cosponsored the exhibition with the Art Guild of St. Philip's Episcopal Church, and the Pauli Murray Project at Duke. The Mary Duke Biddle Foundation provided funding.

When people asked us why we chose to honor Pauli Murray in this way, we often answered that a patchwork quilt was a fitting metaphor for Murray's family history and her work life. From her book *Proud Shoes: The Story of an American Family*, we learn that Murray was descended from black, white, and Native American people. First published in the 1950s, the book reads as though it were written last week. She details her ancestors. One set of great grandparents included a white slaveholder in Orange County, North Carolina, who raped a woman enslaved to his family. The child born of that violent union was Murray's maternal grandmother, Cornelia Smith, who married Robert Fitzgerald, an educator who came to North Carolina after the civil war to aid the emerging black community. His parents were a bi-racial farming couple from Delaware and Maryland. No one wanted to discuss that kind of family history in 1950, not black people and not white people, but that didn't stop Murray from researching and writing a brilliant book about her not-so-unusual American family.

I've just finished reading Murray's autobiography, *Pauli Murray* (formerly published as *Song in a Weary Throat*) and am stunned by her brilliance, the obstacles she faced, and her perseverance. Murray was the first African American to apply to the Graduate School at UNC and was turned down because of her race. As a brilliant student and a descendant of people who had endowed the university, Murray thought she should be admitted to school, but no. She graduated from Howard Law School at the top of her class, which should have entitled her to a yearlong fellowship to Harvard Law School, but Harvard wouldn't take her because she was female. In her fifties, she earned an advanced law degree from Yale. Men who received the same degree got teaching jobs in the best law schools in the country, but law schools weren't yet open to having women on the faculty. Murray was eventually hired by Brandeis in 1968 to teach race and law in the undergraduate college, only to run headlong into students in the Black Power movement and find herself at odds with the very people she had designed her life to serve. She attended seminary in her sixties, was one of the first Episcopal women to be ordained, and was the very first African American woman ordained to the Episcopal priesthood.

Born in Baltimore, Maryland, on November 20, 1910, Pauli Murray grew up with relatives in Durham, North Carolina. That's why Durham has been celebrating her centennial this fall. Watch for Pauli Murray events throughout the coming year. To find more about the various threads of this remarkable woman's life, read *Proud Shoes* or *Pauli Murray*, Google her, or see paulimurrayproject.org.

Volume 31, Number 4, December 2010

SPRING

Friends and I were making art together one January afternoon this year. I was painting valentines, and RCWMS board member Jenny Graves was working on a collage. When she finished, she held it up and said, "I don't know if I even like this." I made my usual comment that making things is much more important than liking them and said I hoped she was glad she had made something. When I looked more closely, I noticed that all of the images in Jenny's collage were reaching up and pointed that out. Someone asked, "Do you know what you are reaching for?" Jenny looked at us knowingly but didn't say.

As spring approaches, the energy of the earth seems to be reaching up and out toward the returning sun. In early February, I brushed away leaves to find crocuses about to bloom by the back steps at home. By the end of the month, daffodil leaves are tall and green and the first yellow blooms have opened. The energy in the earth is inviting me to move away the dead leaves of winter and make room for whatever's coming.

That's what got a hold on me one morning recently. I was happily sitting at my desk at home getting ready to write, when I noticed a particularly dusty spot beside the desk lamp. Since I didn't have to hurry out until after lunchtime, I grabbed a rag from the laundry room and dusted the patch. Then I saw another one. Before I knew it, I had hauled the vacuum upstairs, moved piles of books and papers out into the hall, and given my small study a good cleaning. Pleased with my efforts, I swiped my dust cloth across the window blinds and was horrified by the thick layer of dust it collected. Like a woman possessed, I stuck the fluffy brush attachment onto the end of the vacuum cleaner wand and passed it back and forth until the blinds on all three windows were clean. I wanted to jump back, shout "Ta da!" and wait for the applause.

The only trouble is that what I was doing wasn't writing. According to *The War of Art* by Steven Pressfield, it was merely resistance. That may be true, but it was such a useful kind of resistance, and my theory of cleaning includes going with the energy when it shows up, because it doesn't appear that often. I'm not sure that a clean study makes my writing any better, but it certainly gives me a feeling of relief to have eliminated most of the piles. I no longer spend extra energy glancing at them and worrying about whether there's something in one of them that needs my attention.

Sometimes, I suspect that "being organized" has become a religion in this country. If not a religion, it has certainly become a big business. Eric Abrahamson and David H. Freedman write in *A Perfect Mess* that household and office organizers now have professional organizations and command good pay. Though everyone deserves to make a living— and I commend the ingenuity of the organizers—the authors suggest that the instructions the professionals offer are pretty close to the ones I heard from my mother, "Pick up your toys, and let's give some of the old ones away."

I've been joking that I have a new organizing system this year. I say I'm trying to be as inefficient and disorganized as possible. (Cleaning during writing may even qualify.) It might be that I'm approaching sixty years of age, but moving quickly, doing as many things as possible, and being a whiz-bang at all of it has lost its appeal.

I find that if I move more slowly, schedule fewer hours during the day, and do less, I feel better and am happier. I also notice that by being less "efficient," there's more room for things like a conversation with a friend I might bump into. When I'm less hurried, I'm more likely to take in the color of the sky or the feel of the air around me. When I move too fast, I get cranky and irritable and wind up contributing very little to the wellbeing of the planet.

I want to stop thinking of cleanliness as right up there next to godliness, and I want to stop silently berating myself and others when our living or working spaces get messy. I don't want to live or work in dirty, cluttered spaces, but after all these years, it's pretty clear that my home and office will rarely look like a magazine cover. (My mother's still does.)

The authors of *A Perfect Mess* suggest that the time it takes to keep perfect order may not, in fact, be worth what it would cost for most of us. Perhaps we should use our time for other activities, like making art. Come to think of it, most of the artists I know spend more time making art than organizing their art spaces. Of course, one has to stop periodically to clean up a little, or else there's no room for making art. But who said an art room needed to be as clean, bright, and orderly as an operating room? A certain amount of messiness might even encourage random flashes of creativity.

Don't get me wrong. I don't want to live and work in chaos, but a certain loose ordering of our spaces might be good for us humans. I think I'd like for the spaces around me to be more like my garden.

I've now been messing around in the same garden for nineteen years. I want the garden to be a joy, not a job. My flower garden is in the backyard, which is actually a good place for it. There's sun back there, and people on the street don't have to look at it during the months when it is a little unsightly. I've known people who wanted their flower gardens to be showcases and could make them that way. I just want enough flowers during the warm months of the year that there are blossoms to cut and bring into the house. And my husband, who has serious farmer genes, wants some ground to dig in, room to plant a few things, and something to chop down periodically.

I think of the garden as a kind of recreational therapy. My relationship with it is that I get to play there, it gets to surprise me, and together sometimes we make something beautiful. It needs just enough order for the new energy, ideas, and desires of spring to be able to push through into the light of ever-warming days.

Volume 32, Number 1, March, 2011

AT LONG LAST

I was ordained to the Presbyterian ministry twenty-nine years ago. At the time, I was living in Greensboro with my partner Katherine and working two jobs, as a campus minister at UNC Greensboro and as the Director of the Resource Center for Women and Ministry in the South. My presbytery didn't exactly know that I was a lesbian. They didn't ask and I didn't say.

That was 1982. I had been out of seminary for five years, and it took me all that time to jump through the Presbyterian hoops to be ordained—as a woman, never mind about the rest of it. I went on being a campus minister for a few more years and then switched to just one job, the one with RCWMS, which I still have. I also went on having a female partner until 1990, when I took up with men again.

On the 10th day of May, 2011, as I waited for the last necessary presbytery to approve a Presbyterian Church (USA) amendment that would remove the barriers to the ordination of openly GLBT (gay, lesbian, bisexual, and transgendered) people in our communion, my mind wandered through the stories of friends. Some of my gay and lesbian colleagues kept their mouths shut about their relationships, about their families. Some gave up their ordinations, choosing to be clear, well-integrated, and open about their lives. Some left the denomination altogether and found homes in places like the United Church of Christ, which had given up crucifying and persecuting people based on their sexual orientation.

For those who chose to keep going, remaining ordained members of a denomination that was uncomfortable with their presence, things got stickier. By 1997 and the passage of the "fidelity and chastity" amendment to the *Book of Order*, GLBT ministers and elders were formally out of compliance. Said amendment required fidelity in marriage and celibacy in singleness of Presbyterian clergy and elders. Since GLBT people couldn't be legally married at that point, it left them outside the door, except for those who chose celibacy.

It is that amendment that was being "undone" on May 10, and for that I wanted to shout, "Alleluia!" What we should want of people in leadership is for them to be open, honest, and faithful. We want to teach young people mutual respect and to not take advantage of those who are younger, smaller, or in any way weaker. Sexuality can and should be an expression of love, not of power. Sexual orientation should not be the issue; the quality and equality of relationships should be.

We are a rugged lot, we Presbyterians. We often stay and fight it out. (Perhaps you've heard of the Hatfields and the McCoys. They were our folks.) I've been so proud of GLBT Presbyterians and their allies who didn't give up. We've stayed in the church vowing to change the rules. The debates have become more respectful over the last three decades. The number of people on our side of the issue has continued to increase, and I had almost come to believe I would live to see the day come. But then, just moments before the last needed presbytery began its meeting, I had butterflies in my stomach.

On another exciting day long ago, the day I graduated from seminary, I turned to friends and said, "They'll be sorry." As I watched older people rankle at the idea of GLBT clergy, I said, "They'll age out." In May, on the brink of my sixtieth birthday and what felt like the authorization of my ordination, I just wanted to say, "Thank you."

I am so grateful to the scores of people who have stayed with this church family (the PCUSA) long enough to see this issue a little further down the road. That's a mighty fine example of fidelity in my book.

When we heretics finally get our way, I guess we don't get to be heretics anymore. We get to take up the rank and file of regular, imperfect, sinful people of the church. We also get to remember that we are what there is, we are the stuff God has to work with. We are who there is to do God's work in the world. And there is much more work to do.

To all those who have kept the faith, thank you. You have made me proud to be a Presbyterian.

Volume 32, Number 2, June, 2011

WATER

We've had a really dry summer here in central North Carolina. My garden looks pretty sad—a few scraggly tomato plants, a couple of gasping basil plants, and some dried up echinacea. But I also have a dozen large pots of brightly blooming flowers. The flowers in the pots are happy, because I water them almost every day.

Watering is pleasant if I do it early in the day and also because I have turned it into a game. I try to see if I can water the pots in front of the house and in the backyard without turning on the hose. I get water from three barrels that collect rain water that pours off the garage when it rains, and I get water from the bucket underneath the condensate drain at the back of the house.

I think everyone knows about rain barrels by now. I'm here to tell you that if you live where it actually rains, you don't have to hook up any fancy downspouts to collect water in a barrel. You can be a lazy gardener like me. Just stick the thing under the eves where water pours off, and there you have it—water in a container to use on your garden.

Not everyone has discovered air conditioning as a source of water. You may not even have thought of catching the drips that hit the ground somewhere outside your house or apartment. You might be suspicious, as I am, of anything liquid that comes out of a machine, but I checked it out and it is basically just sweat. It's water that is in the air and turns into liquid in the cooling process. I don't completely understand how it works, but I can see the water dripping out of the black rubber hose. On a typical summer day, that slow dripping fills a five-gallon bucket twice a day. Though I'm still skittish about putting that water on things I'm going to eat, I'm very happy to use it on the flowers.

My neighbors across the street dug up their driveway this summer and installed an underground water storage tank to collect rain water and air conditioning condensate. The experts told them that they could collect up to forty gallons of water a day from the air conditioning system in their big old house. That's 1,200 gallons a month. I was stunned. They have a substantial vegetable garden that has been taking thousands of gallons of water a month. It's not just the cost, it's that there is water around if we catch it.

One warning: there are places in the country where catching rainwater is illegal, mostly in perpetually dry areas. If you live in one of these, you already know about this caveat, because the rainwater laws have been in place for over 100 years. If you don't live in a dry state, you can just let your mouth gape open as you consider the fact that someone could legislate against your catching water that falls on your house from the sky. But there you have it. Water is a precious resource and if lots of people in Denver caught the water that fell on their property, the city wouldn't have enough to go around for the everyone else. (Colorado has recently made it legal to catch rainwater in some places.)

Meanwhile, do yourself and everyone else a favor and put a rain barrel or at least a bucket out in the yard. Since rain falls on the good and evil alike, you might as well enjoy this freely given gift.

Volume 32, Number 3, September, 2011

OCCUPY

Pictures of UC Davis police officers pepper-spraying protesters in the face left many of us with a deep sense of moral outrage. The images reminded me of police violence at antiwar protests decades ago. I was a freshman in college in 1970 when National Guardsmen shot and killed demonstrators at Kent State. I didn't think that the use of such force against protesters was appropriate forty years ago and I don't think it is now.

I have been following the Occupy Wall Street movement with great interest. I was unhappy about the bailout of big banks a couple of years ago and the redistribution of wealth over decades. Enough pressure from the movement could shore up regulations, strengthen legislation, and eventually reduce inequities.

I was shocked by the treatment of protesters in New York, Berkeley, and Oakland and surprised that New York City Mayor Bloomberg had the right, under the Patriot Act, to delay the press in publishing pictures of injured protesters. But when my friend Jen Schradie was arrested on the Friday after Thanksgiving while taking pictures inside a Raleigh mall, I got really mad.

Jen was visiting from Oakland, California, and attended an Occupy Raleigh protest at the mall. From reports, it seems a small group entered the food court. One man addressed the crowded eating area, saying things like "give thanks, not stuff" and "stop corporate greed." Others joined in and then police arrested six of them.

Jen's charges included, "…intentionally cause a public disturbance at CRABTREE VALLEY MALL, by making utterances, intended and plainly likely to provoke immediate violent retaliation and thereby cause a breach of the peace. The acts of the defendant were directed toward CROWD IN FOOD COURT and consisted of remarks about the OCCUPY RALEIGH PROTEST." She was reportedly taking video with her iPhone when arrested, an odd "breach of the peace." Though large open areas at a mall may look like public spaces, they aren't. They are private property owned by large corporations. If you aren't doing what the owners want, you can be arrested for trespassing or breach of the peace.

By November 26, there had been 4,784 arrests connected with Occupy activities around the country (a Facebook page keeps count). The arrests made me wonder about the state of our civil rights and civil liberties. I wondered whether it was legal for UC Davis police to use pepper spray on people sitting quietly on the ground, so I did some looking on the Internet. It turns out it's *not* legal. Several months before the events at Davis, the 9th Circuit Court of Appeals ruled in a case about a similar incident and found that "the use of pepper spray on the protesters' eyes and faces was plainly in excess of the force necessary under the circumstances, and no reasonable officer could have concluded otherwise."

Perhaps the UC Davis police were unaware of the new standards or mistook the seated students for a dangerous mob. In fact, truth spoken to power often provokes intimidation, and as North Carolina activist Sr. Evelyn Mattern used to say, "The price of freedom is constant vigilance." So, stay calm and keep your cameras on!

Volume 32, Number 4, December, 2011

SIXTY

I attended a sixtieth birthday celebration for a friend in late January. Guests were invited to bring poems, songs, skits, or readings for the occasion, which got me started thinking about what advice I might give now that I've been sixty for several months. Others had offered me wisdom and warnings as I approached this particular bend in the road we call life. One colleague warned that she suddenly lost interest in her job when she turned sixty. While I am still willing to do my job, I have noticed some other changes.

First of all, I don't seem to want to put on "real" clothes very often anymore. I seem happier wearing my cropped black yoga pants and sneakers every day. My yoga pants have a loose elastic waist that doesn't squeeze me and since they are stretchy pants, they don't grab me anywhere. I guess the real truth is that I want to wear clothes that feel like pajamas. I'd rather they not look like pajamas, as I'm not yet ready to be that much of an oddity.

I will admit that because I stay home in the mornings to write, many a weekday lunch hour arrives to find me still in my blue bathrobe. My husband and I have a joke: sometimes when he comes home for lunch, I holler down from upstairs, "Look out! Here comes the blue bathrobe bandit." You have to be there for it to be funny, but it amuses me. Annie Lamott says that when she was young, she wanted her father "to have a regular job where he put on a necktie and went off somewhere with the other fathers," instead of staying home in his slippers like a mental patient. I sometimes feel that way about myself.

In addition to wearing my bathrobe or yoga clothes all the time, I seem to be changing my schedule. This fall and winter, I find myself walking with my friend Jenny at 2:00 in the afternoon or racing to the YMCA to try to get in a swim before 3:30 when they close the pool for an hour and a half. Serious people exercise before or after work. At 3:00 p.m. the only people in the pool are...*old*.

A few weeks ago as I was splashing around doing my exercises from water aerobics class, I noticed that the woman in the lane next to me had finished her laps and was swimming toward the ladder. I watched her climb carefully out of the pool. Later, when I hopped out of the pool without using the ladder, I wondered whether I was just showing off. Was I trying to deny my age? After all, I WAS there in the middle of the afternoon with the retirement crowd.

People say, "You don't look sixty," so often to me that it's not really even entertaining any more. I didn't look sixteen when I was sixteen either. At least people aren't trying to tell me I look twelve anymore. When I'm with my young friends (the ones thirty and under) I often forget that I'm twice their age.

Here's the truth: this is what sixty looks and feels like now.

And I'm glad to have friends who are ahead of me on the path who are aging gracefully and happy to have friends my age with whom I can try to figure all this out.

Volume 33, Number 1, March, 2012

NUNS

When RCWMS began thirty-five years ago, there were few Protestant women in formal ministry in North Carolina. Some of our early role models were Roman Catholics nuns, who were readily apparent even in the South. I first noticed them in campus ministry, in academia, and in social justice work. I was grateful to the Catholic sisters even then for blazing trails, for being strong, independent professional women, and for creating new definitions of community beyond the convent walls.

That was 1977, a dozen years after the Second Vatican Council. Many nuns had shed their habits, "women religious" like Evelyn Mattern who worked in social justice for the Catholic Diocese and then for the North Carolina Council of Churches. I remember noticing her tasteful dark blue dress the first time I met Evelyn. She had left her canonical order to help form Sisters for Christian Community, a new community outside the traditional structures. Keeping vows of poverty, chastity, and obedience to the community, this group of women religious went right on with their calling to religious life and with their work in the world, but without priests and bishops breathing down their necks.

Some women left the sisterhood altogether, but many remained in communities under the control of local priests and bishops, giving faithful service for low wages, while running schools, hospitals, and parishes.

Being in religious life is not as popular as it once was. At the time of Vatican II (mid-1960s) there were 180,000 women religious in the US. Today there are less than 70,000, with a median age of over seventy. It is these faithful, stalwart, selfless servants of the church who came under attack in April 2012.

In April, the Vatican Congregation for the Doctrine of the Faith issued a condemnation of the Leadership Conference of Women Religious (LCWR), the main umbrella organization of Catholic sisters in the US, and appointed a conservative archbishop to oversee the organization's activities. The Vatican justified its takeover by accusing the LCWR of challenging church teachings and of being radical feminists.

The response to the Vatican crackdown was swift and the response of progressive US Catholics was outrage. Feminist scholar of American Catholicism Marian Ronan wrote, "The idea of these utterly dedicated and highly educated women coming under this kind of attack for exercising their freedom of conscience by sometimes disagreeing with the American bishops drives me nuts."

There you have it. The women didn't agree with the men in charge and got slammed for it. Ronan points out that the conflict between the men and the women is age old. (See her blog, marianronan.wordpress.com.)

Commentators have suggested that the current disagreements between the sisters and the Vatican include opinions on homosexuality, same-sex marriage, the ordination of women, and a whole range of family planning issues—from birth control to abortion to Obama's healthcare plan, which included some provisions for contraception. A Catholic social justice lobby that nuns started forty years ago, NETWORK, supported Obama's plan while US bishops opposed it.

But why attack the sisters now? Catholic feminist theologian Mary Hunt suggests a tactical maneuver. "How dare the very men who preside over a church in utter disgrace due to sexual misconduct and cover-ups by bishops try to distract from their own problems by creating new ones for women religious?"

Whatever the reasons, the result is to drive a deeper wedge between the Vatican and US Catholics. As Hunt says, "...truth is, most Catholics no longer look to Rome for guidance on our personal lives." Polls show eighty-two percent of US Catholics find birth control morally acceptable. Since the Vatican is not known for backing down, there's no telling how this conflict will go. There have been big splashes in the press, rallies and protests outside meetings of bishops, and the upcoming meeting of the LCWR is bound to be exciting.

Feminist and former LCWR President Joan Chittister offered one suggestion, "to disband canonically and regroup as an unofficial interest group." It's certainly the approach taken by Sisters for Christian Community and by many American Catholics who find ways to stay connected to the church while living their own versions of faithful modern lives.

Once again, I find myself grateful to the brave sisters for being fine role models. I trust they will continue to figure out how to make more space for women to be heard and for justice to be lived out even in the midst of regressive, hierarchical, patriarchal, authoritarian structures.

Volume 33, Number 2, June 2012

35 YEARS

While studying at Duke Divinity School in the mid-1970s, I served a year as the director of the divinity school's Women's Center. There I learned that some women students were having a hard time in their ministerial internships. Some were belittled, some harassed, and some were simply lonely. I also noticed that there wasn't much support available for women in ministry and those entering ministry.

The summer after I graduated from seminary, I set out to discover what my female colleagues needed. I had a vague notion of creating some sort of women's center, of saying, "I'm interested in feminism and religion; is anyone else?" My women friends who were serving local parishes said they wanted someone to care that they were out there, to create ways for them to get together with other women in ministry, and to provide resources to support and encourage them.

With only a vague sense of what we might do to meet these needs, I hired a lawyer and set up the Resource Center for Women and Ministry in the South. That was 1977. Thirty-five years later, we've done all kinds of things. We've hosted conferences and workshops on feminist theology, economic justice, women and violence, and creativity and spirituality. We've offered retreats on writing, meditation, aging, and caring for ourselves. We've sponsored art exhibitions and published newsletters, books, music CDs, and DVDs.

In the last ten years our work has focused on creativity, spirituality, and social justice.

CREATIVITY & WRITING

In 2002, Nancy Peeler Keppel approached RCWMS with an offer. She said she would send some money our way if we would do some programing on faith and the arts. She was particularly interested in writing. She and her family foundation provided substantial support for our writing program for several years, which gave it time to take root and grow strong. The program now offers resources to writers that range from workshops for those new to writing, to weeklong retreats at the beach, to the publication of books. We have also offered workshops, classes, and ongoing writing groups, an annual essay contest, grants to several writers, and advice and encouragement to many more.

We have been involved in publishing several books. We helped with the production of *God Speaks, Women Respond*, a collection of essays by United Church of Christ women in ministry. RCWMS published *Enough Room*, a book of poetry by Sue Versényi; two collections of my essays entitled *25 Years in the Garden* and *35 Years on the Path*; and *Good Busy: Productivity, Procrastination, and the Endless Pursuit of Balance*, by Julia Scatliff O'Grady.

CREATIVITY & ART

In 2006, the Resource Center designed and produced "Art & the Feminine Divine," an exhibition of more than 175 works of art by 100 North Carolina artists. The art filled five venues in Durham, North Carolina, and was accompanied by a yearlong series of workshops and concerts focused on feminine images of the divine. Hundreds of people attended the exhibition and events, making it the single largest effort the organization had ever undertaken.

We have also sponsored smaller exhibitions. Two of these were one-woman shows by Carole Baker. "Mary: The Paper Doll Project" was a 2009 exhibition of life-size, interactive images of Mary, the mother of Jesus, painted by the artist. The freestanding images, each from a different branch of Christianity, had clothes that visitors could switch among the various "dolls." "The Confessional," a large-scale installation, opened during Lent 2010. Viewers entered a constructed environment where they could reflect on themes of brokenness, healing, and the radical practice of forgiveness.

RCWMS has produced two documentary films. (Both are available on DVD from RCWMS.) *Meinrad Craighead: Praying with Images* (2009) traces the life and work of a visionary artist and former nun who lives in Albuquerque, New Mexico. Executive producer Amy Kellum spent four years raising money, traveling with Meinrad, and making this first-rate hour-long film. Before she was done, Amy had raised more than $100,000 from foundations and more than 500 individuals. Openings were held in Durham and in Albuquerque. As of this writing, 1,500 DVDs of the documentary are in circulation. To learn more, visit www.meinradproject.com.

The second documentary, *Blackbirds, Bottle Caps, and Broken Records: Environmental Artist Bryant Holsenbeck at Work* (2010) shares the story of a remarkably creative woman whose work encourages people to notice all the trash we create and throw away and inspires them to protect the natural world. Margaret Morales did a wonderful job making the film, which premiered on Bryant's birthday in August 2010. When Bryant shows it to school groups, the children think she is a movie star. She is. More at www.bryantholsenbeck.com.

SPIRITUALITY

RCWMS has been encouraging women and men in their spiritual development for more than three decades. In the last decade, we have hosted winter interfaith celebrations, and have offered workshops on yoga and meditation and retreats on creativity and spirituality. At present, we pay special attention to feminist spiritual direction, to spirituality for elder women, and to Tara, the beloved female buddha of Tibet.

Rachael Wooten, a Jungian analyst in Raleigh, North Carolina, served on the RCWMS Board for six years (2003–2008), and during that time she taught us about Tara. RCWMS began to sponsor programs on Tara, which included a workshop and three weekend retreats at the beach, all led by Rachael.

I didn't know there was a female buddha until I met Rachael Wooten. Did you? Tara is often depicted sitting atop a lotus blossom with her left leg folded in the meditation position and her right foot extended, a position that indicates she is ready to come to our aid. In fact, it is said that when we call, she is already here. I wish I had grown up believing there was a female incarnation of the divine who was just waiting to come to my aid. (Thank goodness I did learn that some of my female friends would lend assistance.)

Rachael began studying the practices devoted to the Twenty-one Taras while she was training at the Jung Institute in Switzerland in the 1990s. A few years later she helped her Tibetan teacher, Lodro Tulku Rinpoche, translate the practices into English. Once back in the States, she organized women's meditation groups to use the practices. With the inspiration and help of Beth Hardin, a member of one of the groups, she developed a set of devotional cards, *The Tara Cards*, and is now writing a book to accompany them.

FEMINIST SPIRITUAL DIRECTION

RCWMS has long been interested in feminism and spirituality, and for the last few years we have been exploring feminist spiritual direction. Spiritual direction is a covenant relationship between fellow travelers on a journey of faith, mindfully and humbly conducted in the presence of the Spirit. Feminist spiritual direction gives special attention to the character of being "woman" in our culture and seeks to empower women—lesbian, bisexual, and straight—in their unique spiritual journeys, and thus in the rest of their lives. In its emphasis on women's wholeness, feminist spiritual direction implicitly seeks justice and wholeness for all of God's people and creation.

Kaudie McLean, PhD, has recently joined RCWMS as our spiritual director. A writer, editor, artist, and certified spiritual director, she is leading our feminist spiritual direction program. To explore spiritual direction with her, contact: kaudiemc@earthlink.net.

ELDER WOMEN

Anita McLeod has developed the Elder Women project out of her desire to encourage elder women to be a force for peace and justice in the world. A semi-retired health educator and former Chair of the Board of RCWMS, Anita started leading menopause workshops more than twenty years ago. She has partnered with RCWMS in the last decade to lead "Wise Choices," retreats for women over sixty, and is now developing a wide variety of programs for elder women.

Anita likes to quote a Hopi prophecy: "When the grandmothers speak, the earth will heal." She wants to help elder women claim their wisdom, lead with their hearts, and repair their sacred connection with the earth. She points out that more women are entering their sixties, seventies, and eighties with better health, higher levels of education, greater work experience, and more resources than ever before in history. These women have time and choices their mothers and grandmothers never dreamed of. The question now is how to "give back."

RCWMS received a $20,000 grant from the Kalliopeia Foundation in May 2012 for the Elder Women project. Funds will be used to expand our programs that encourage the spiritual and creative development of elder women.

PAULI MURRAY

In November 2010, people in Durham, North Carolina, celebrated the centennial of the birth of the Rev. Dr. Pauli Murray, a tireless advocate for civil rights, workers' rights, and women's rights. She was a lawyer, scholar, author, poet, and university professor, a founder of the National Organization for Women (NOW), and eventually the first African American woman to be ordained as an Episcopal priest. Born in Baltimore, Maryland, Murray grew up in Durham. In the 1950s, she published *Proud Shoes: The Story of an American Family*, a remarkable book about her childhood in Durham and her interracial ancestry.

Murray wrote, "It has taken me almost a lifetime to discover that true emancipation lies in the acceptance of the whole past." As part of the centennial celebration, RCWMS organized an exhibition of quilts and other textile art at St. Philip's Episcopal Church in Durham. We called it "Strength from All My Roots." The Mary Duke Biddle Foundation provided funding, and the exhibition was cosponsored by the St. Philip's Art Guild and the Pauli Murray Project at Duke University. For more information about Pauli Murray, visit www.paulimurrayproject.org.

THE FUTURE

In the last decade we have produced large public events, hosted small workshops and retreats, and published books and films, all focused on creativity, spirituality, justice, and equality. When I add it all up, it has been nothing less than remarkable. Those of us around RCWMS sometimes look at one another and ask, "How did we pull that off?" But then I've been wondering that since the beginning of the organization.

I am amazed that thirty-five years after it began, RCWMS is still here, and that I still love being involved in it. Part of what makes it such interesting work is that RCWMS operates by looking around to see what is needed and we invent things we wish were there. We draw on the gifts and inspiration of the people who participate in our programs or serve on our board of trustees. They, and you, will help to create our future. I can't wait to see what will come next.

Volume 33, Number 3, September 2012

Copies of this book may be ordered from:
The Resource Center for Women and Ministry in the South, Inc.
1202 Watts Street
Durham, North Carolina 27701
919-683-1236
rcwmsnc@aol.com
www.rcwms.org

154